THE OTHER TITANIC

THE OTHER TITANIC

SIMON MARTIN

DAVID & CHARLES

Newton Abbot   London   North Pomfret (Vt)

British Library Cataloguing in Publication Data

Martin, Simon
    The other Titanic.
    1. Salvage — Scotland — Foula
    2. Oceanic *(Ship)*
    I. Title
    914.113'5   VK1491

    ISBN 0-7153-7755-8

Typeset by Unwin Brothers Limited
The Gresham Press Old Woking Surrey
and printed in Great Britain
by Biddles Limited Guildford Surrey
for David & Charles (Publishers) Limited
Brunel House Newton Abbot Devon

Published in the United States of America
by David & Charles Inc
North Pomfret Vermont 05053 USA

Contents

Acknowledgements 6

Introduction 7

1 Why 'The Other Titanic'? 9

2 The *Oceanic* After Sixty Years 42

3 Salvors in Court 81

4 Peat Banks and Propeller Blades 97

5 Lifting a Liner Piece by Piece 123

6 Island Wedding 148

7 The End of *Trygg* 166

8 Success and Near-disaster 186

Postscript 195

Appendix: Salvage Report by Alec Crawford 199

Index 205

Acknowledgements

I should like to thank the following for allowing me to use their photographs: Harland & Wolff, Belfast, Merseyside County Museums, the Public Records Office, Alison McLeay, my brother Colin Martin and Robert Johnson. The underwater plans were drawn up by Alec Crawford, and the other drawings were done by Alison McLeay. All the underwater photographs were taken by Alec Crawford. I am also grateful to Alec Crawford for the loan of his salvage diaries.

Finally, I should like to say a special 'thank you' to the Foula folk, who accepted us as their own.

Introduction

This is the story of a most unlikely diving expedition in one of the remotest and bleakest spots in the British Isles. In most expeditions there is sponsorship, a fund-raising campaign, cascades of publicity, and months if not years of careful planning. Our effort was nothing like that. If it had been planned and discussed it would undoubtedly have been dismissed as a hopeless dream even before it started. A short trip for a special 'fun' dive became a major project over a six-year period; our two-man expedition just happened.

Over those years Alec Crawford and I salvaged more than 200 tons of valuable non-ferrous metals worth many thousands of pounds from the forgotten wreck of the *Oceanic*, the liner which was a contemporary of, and even more magnificent than, the celebrated *Titanic*. You may well ask how two divers, with no experience in large-scale salvage, came to be working on the wreck of one of the world's most impressive ships—a wreck which had been declared 'undiveable' by professionals and which had lain for half a century, undisturbed and forgotten, in a wellnigh inaccessible spot and in a fierce tide race of allegedly 12 knots. The answer is that it was pure chance.

In 1973 Alec and I had been teamed up for a year, though we had each worked previously with other diving partners. We weren't interested in oil-rig contracts, or in harbour, pier or pipeline work. Like thousands of other divers who enjoy the sport in wetsuit and aqualung, we dived because we enjoyed it, but we also had to earn our living from it—to that extent we were professionals—and we did so mainly by recovering non-ferrous fittings of copper, brass and gunmetal from shallow-water steamship wrecks.

We had had some successes, but latterly we had been forced to settle, for a time at least, for the simple, unspectacular but steady cash of clam diving in the Outer Hebrides. In terms of excitement it's rather like picking potatoes, but we stuck it for a winter because the work put our finances in reasonably good shape. We were, however, far from making our fortunes, and we planned one final summer season of full-time diving before returning to our respective trades of farming and journalism.

That summer was spent far to the north on the tiny Shetland island of Fair Isle, where Alec and I had dived previously. Fair Isle is an island of shipwrecks, and we visited many of them, spending some time working on the remains of the Spanish Armada flagship, *El Gran Grifon*, under the direction of my brother Colin, now director of the Institute of Maritime Archaeology of St Andrews University.

Often, once the day's diving was completed, we were entertained by island friends in their croft houses, and it was after dinner one night at Quoy, the island home of Stewart and Triona Thomson, that we flicked through the pages of a book about Foula, and read of the wreck of the *Oceanic*.

The record of our diving experiences on that wreck begins in Chapter 2, but this book would be sadly incomplete without an account of this great, forgotten liner and how she came to her disastrous end in 1914.

1
Why
'The Other Titanic'?

Ever since records have been kept, there have been hundreds of thousands of shipwrecks all over the world. Each one has its own tale, sometimes of heroism, sometimes of tragedy; of miraculous rescue or appalling loss of life; of fortunes saved from the sea or lost and awaiting some future finder. The tales of many wreckings have been amply recorded, while thousands of others have disappeared into history. But ask the average layman in almost any country in the world to name just one shipwreck, and the chances are he will immediately mention the *Titanic*, the 'unsinkable' ship that sank all the same on her maiden voyage after colliding with an iceberg.

With dreams of salvage, the *Titanic* has also become the epitome of all shipwrecks. Though the wreck lies more than 2 miles deep, and even oil-rig divers have not yet descended to a quarter of that depth, it is just feasible—if money were no object whatsoever—that the *Titanic* could be lifted. The Americans raised most of a Russian submarine from a greater depth than this, but it was really a multi-million dollar public-relations exercise to prove they could do something the Russians could not.

As far as economic considerations go, work on the *Titanic* has always been a non-starter. Yet many a 'Salvage the *Titanic*' scheme has been launched, and incredible ideas are hatched every year by utterly inexperienced 'salvors'. Businessmen, far too shrewd ever to be taken in by a dubious stock exchange deal, are still lured by the impossible dream and pour funds into ventures that never get under way.

Any dreamer, even someone obviously broke and unrealistic, has only to mention that he plans to raise the *Titanic* to have the world's press come running.

Ping-pong balls are often mentioned as a 'secret' weapon for the raising—the fact that pressure would cause them to collapse only a few feet down is conveniently forgotten. The ship's model, in a Liverpool museum along with the models of other famous White Star liners, is often studied by earnest young men who carefully note points where lifting wires could be attached, completely ignoring the size of winches that would be required to lift just two-and-a-half miles of *wire*, let alone 50,000 tons of ship as well.

But the charisma of the name lives on. Every diver who has ever lived must have been asked at least once by an onlooker, 'Well—when are you going to lift the *Titanic*?'. This palatial vessel, with her gilded cherubs, stained glass, marble staircases and luxurious furnishings, remains an irresistible treasure.

In realistic terms, the value of a ship like the *Titanic* lies in non-ferrous fittings such as her bronze propellers, the steam condensers, pumps, bearings, valves and pipes. It is ridiculous to talk about such recoveries from that depth; the shipwreck would have to lie in shallow water to make salvage economic.

Throughout the world there are thousands of divers, both amateur and professional, who regularly dive around the 100 ft mark. Tell them that an older and slightly smaller sister of the *Titanic*, with virtually the same value and design of engine-room fittings, lies in British waters well within that depth, and they would stare at you in disbelief. They would be even more surprised if you went on to suggest that such a wreck had been ignored for more than half a century.

A ship with fittings even more sumptuous than the *Titanic*, with not so much as a scrap of metal taken off her—how could such a ship have escaped the hordes of present-day divers, and the expert salvage men of the 1920s and 1930s, when many an amazing salvage feat was accomplished?

This is the story of that ship—the fabulous *Oceanic*.

Thomas Henry Ismay, one of the greatest men in nineteenth-century shipbuilding and founder of the famous White Star Line, was determined that his prosperous and influential company would fittingly mark the end of a century that had seen momentous developments in shipbuilding techniques. He would construct the most magnificent ship ever built. Money was to be no object—the then massive sum of nearly £1 million was earmarked for the project—and everything had to be of the best, even down to the smallest door-knobs, in what was to be the biggest ship in the world.

Nearly 30 years before, Ismay had formed the Oceanic Steam Navigation Co—more often known as the White Star Line after its house-flag—and under his astute guidance it rapidly grew in stature in a highly competitive field. By 1897 he was taking a less active role in the running of the line. He left day-to-day business to his two sons, though he remained as company chairman, but he masterminded the conception of the finest ship in the world, a ship that was to be a monument (and later a memorial) to himself and his line, a ship that for years was to retain the title of 'Queen of the Seas'.

The company's first steamship (by this time broken up) had taken the company name, *Oceanic*, and this latest ship was to be the second to carry the title. In the fiercely competitive and cut-throat North Atlantic shipping trade, rivals had thrashed every last fraction of a knot out of overworked engines in efforts to achieve the fastest crossing between England and the United States and thus gain the coveted Blue Riband. However, with the crossing time now generally down to less than a week, Ismay shrewdly decided that he would not concentrate on pure speed. While other lines would vie with one another to knock a few minutes off the crossing time, Ismay's mighty *Oceanic* was unrivalled in the sheer splendour of her lines, presentation, and the utter magnificence of her décor and interior.

The shipping world was astounded when the plans for the ship were announced and her keel was laid in 1897. The interior was to be of such quality that it would have not looked out of place in the finest mansions in England. The first-class berths and rooms were to be decorated in great splendour. No expense was to be spared, and the finest carvings, statues and paintings were to be featured throughout the ship. Even down to such small details as the light fittings (gold-plated) and the first-class lavatories (marble), Ismay's rigid policy of 'nothing but the very finest' was strictly adhered to.

There was no doubt where this splendid ship was to be built—at the yard of the Belfast shipbuilders, Harland & Wolff. For many years there had been close personal and financial links between the two companies, and such was the rapport between them that there were never any problems over the estimating and costing of ships: Harland & Wolff built them, the White Star Line settled the bill. Dealings over many years were completely harmonious. Indeed when Harland & Wolff sent their fiftieth White Star liner down the ways in 1911—the ill-fated *Titanic*—only one White Star steamer had been built in another yard.

Once the keel of the new record-breaker had been laid, construction work had to be delayed for some time while a special 500 ton gantry—again a world-record size—was erected to help in the building. This formed an arch over the ship, travelled on rails, and carried riveting machines. cranes and electric lamps. Although 1,500 men were employed to build her, this number would have been far greater but for the fact that for the first time hydraulic riveting was used in the yard. About 17,000 shell plates, some of them weighing more than 3 tons, were used in the hull. Some of the plates had 900 rivet holes, and 1,700,000 rivets were put in the whole ship, which would have been a superhuman job using the old methods.

The ship herself was just over 700 ft long, with a 68 ft beam and marginally under 50 ft moulded depth. Loaded, the ship would draw about 32 ft of water, while her displacement tonnage was over 30,000 tons. These vital statistics showed a long sleek ship with a narrow beam—lines that were very pleasing to purist eyes. She had fifteen boilers, each weighing nearly 100 tons, and two engines—triple expansion, four cylinder and four-crank-balanced—producing about 28,000 hp. The engines were the largest ever built of her type (there was no turbine), and at full steam the boiler fires would consume no less than 700 tons of coal each day. In such circumstances forty-five stokers would be working at one time. She could carry massive stocks of coal, however, and at 12 knots—her maximum was around 20 knots—she had the capacity of sailing right round the world without re-fuelling.

The *Oceanic* was designed to carry just over 2,000 people on each trip—410 first-class passengers, 300 second-class, and 1,000 third-class or steerage. There were 394 crew members.

Ironically, considering how she was eventually to meet her end, she was designed with extra strength, particularly round her upper works and the bilges. It was thought she would have a greater chance of survival in the case of stranding or collision, and thirteen transverse bulkheads were introduced. Commander C.H. Lightoller, who was the only senior officer to survive the *Titanic* wrecking and who was also to be wrecked on the *Oceanic*, always reckoned that the *Oceanic*, with her strong construction, would have survived the collision with the iceberg which sent the *Titanic* to the bottom.

The launch of the *Oceanic* was a splendid affair. Well over 50,000 people crammed on to every available vantage point—many on the rigging of ships around the harbour, on the dock wharfs and anywhere else overlooking the hull. Five thousand more were accommodated in a specially erected stand, paying 10s each for the privilege, the money going to a Belfast hospital. Ismay had created a strong family feeling in his firm and never forgot his workers: White Star staff, both those who worked ashore and at sea, were—along with their wives—honoured guests.

The launch day, 14 January, 1899, was fine, clear and dry. Just before the hull started to move slowly down the ways, the sun shone out brilliantly, and the magnificent outlines of the new ship were shown to their fullest effect. Unusually, there was no launching ceremony as such, and the wives of the builder and owners sat with the other spectators. This was the glorious culmination of a century of revolutionary changes in shipbuilding technique, and the entire White Star Line rather than one individual was to take the spotlight.

Two rockets were fired as a signal for all the small boats in the river to stand clear. Five minutes later another two rockets were fired to warn the two familiar Mersey tugs, *Pathfinder* and *Wrestler*, to be at the ready. Slowly, almost imperceptibly, the great ship began to move and a cry rose from the excited crowd. 'She's moving!' Tumultuous cheering broke out as she accelerated down the ways, accompanied by the blaring of sirens all along the river. Soon water covered the lower blades of the propellers, which began to turn slowly with the pressure. A heavy wave swept the quay, and hemp ropes cracked like whiplashes as they broke under the strain. They were part of a system of ropes and chains used to slow the ship as she took to the water, and she drew up exactly to plan. The tugs quickly took her under control. The first great moment in the life of any ship was over.

The *Marine Engineer* visited the ship some months later, inspected the sumptuous passenger accommodation, and published a report liberally laced with superlatives:

> The saloon has as many seats as the ship has first class berths, so everyone can dine at the same time. The room is remarkable for its decoration. It is panelled in oak washed with gold, while its saloon dome (designed by a Royal Academician), decorated with allegorical figures, representing Great Britain and the United States and Liverpool and New York, is very beautiful and striking.
>
> The usual interlocking tiles are furnished as a flooring throughout the passages and other parts of the ship, but in the main companion they are laid out in a way not hitherto applied to steamers. Large lozenges of white rubber are at their corners cut into by small black blocks of the same shape. Thus the effect of a marble floor is conveyed to the eye, though noiselessness and the secure foothold are qualities of its own.
>
> The main companion is very fine, well lit from above and roomy. There are striking and massive carved door posts, coloured plain and

white, which lead to the passages at the side of the ship. The magnificent staircase has panels of brilliant Turkey red with gilt designs on them, and this striking effect very much relieves the general view. The library is over the saloon, the dome of the lower apartment forming the centre of the saloon. The carving of the doors, which are of mahogany, and of the panelling, which is of oak, is very fine, while the electric light fittings are plated in gold. The selection of books, both in this room and the second class library, is large and the binding of both sets is reminiscent of the taste of the head of the firm.

The smokeroom is lighted by two domes, one on each side of the middle line of the ship. Its ornamentation is tasteful. The pictures depict various scenes in the life of Columbus, and in the corners are niches containing beautiful Italian figures. The walls are covered with highly embossed leather gilt, and there is a carved mahogany frieze. The ornamentation, both of the frieze and of the stained glass sliding shutters to the side ports, is of sea nymphs.

The staterooms are large and lofty, while the rooms on the upper deck are most luxurious. The arrangements of these vary greatly. Some are panelled in silk cretonne, and there are most elaborate and convenient appliances for washing stands and toilet tables. Some of the rooms are arranged in suites so that the wealthy Americans can have their bed, sitting and bath rooms all together. The general service of baths, lavatories, some of which are marble, and sanitary conveniences is perfect, and the ship is fitted with the usual barber's shop with its electrical appliances.

Crowds thronged the banks of the Mersey for the *Oceanic*'s maiden voyage, though as a precaution the ship didn't come alongside the landing stage since there was the threat of a strike from the firemen, perhaps daunted by the thought of shovelling up to 700 tons of coal each day! Sadly Ismay himself was too ill to make the journey (he had the first of the series of heart attacks that were to kill him soon after the *Oceanic* left port), but nearly 2,000 on board—and countless thousands on the river banks—cheered and celebrated as the ship made her way out to open sea.

Honoured guests were placed in the twenty sumptuous cabins with private baths which in future would be reserved for 'millionaires and star actresses and such as could afford £100-£150 for a single passage across the Atlantic' in a ship described as 'the Hotel Cecil afloat'.

The *Oceanic* had fine weather for the trip, and her passage to New York took 6 days, 2 hours and 27 minutes at an average speed of 19·57 knots. Under the command of a splendid seaman, Captain John G. Cameron, a man who frequently terrified his crew without losing their intense respect, she was never required to develop more than 20,000 of her 28,000 hp, and never rolled more than five degrees throughout her entire trip of 2,780 miles. As in Belfast and Liverpool, she arrived in New York to a rapturous reception. Tug-boat skippers vied for the honour of pulling her into position.

In those days no news was usually good news for shipping lines and the *Oceanic*, without fuss, carried on with her job as mail steamer—one of the main links between Britain and the United States. In her early days she had the reputation of being a lucky ship as no one was killed or even seriously injured during her construction and launch—an unusual occurrence in days when safety standards in shipyards were very lax.

She never attempted to capture any speed records, and reliability and a steady passage became her trademark. White Star business flourished, and travellers quickly realised that the hour or two saved by crossing in a faster steamer was not very important—particularly when they had the chance of a memorable crossing in the sumptuous *Oceanic*.

But even the *Oceanic* had her moments of excitement. Once she was struck by lightning in the Mersey and lost part of her mainmast. On another occasion, while steaming through fog near the Tuskar Rock, off Rosslare, she sliced clean through the coaster *Kincora*, which sank with the loss of seven lives. (Attempts at the Court of Inquiry to saddle the *Oceanic* with the responsibility failed.)

In 1905 a mutiny by some of the firemen was quelled and thirty-three of them were jailed. The firemen often had to work in terrible conditions, but many had been in trouble with the law. Mr William Hood, of Fort Lauderdale in Florida, told me his father was 3rd engineer on the *Oceanic* for thirteen trips in the early years of this century:

'He once remonstrated with a stoker for loafing, and the man tried to hit him with a shovel,' recalled Mr Hood. 'Father felled him, and both men were taken before the captain. The stoker turned out to be a member of the notorious Liverpool gang, the High Rips, and his back bore recent marks of the cat-o'-nine-tails, administered for vicious assaults.' Captain Cameron believed his officer's story, merely suggesting that he didn't hit the stoker so hard next time! It was a tough breed of man that shovelled the coals in the boiler-room of a large steamer.

In 1907 the *Oceanic* switched her English base from Liverpool to Southampton, which she shared with such ships as the *Majestic, Teutonic* and *Adriatic*. Five years later, ironically in the context of the title of this book, she was nearly involved in a collision with the *Titanic*. The *Oceanic* and *St Paul* were lying side by side moored at Southampton. As the *Titanic* was leaving port she had to make a slight turn, which meant she had to come a touch astern on her port engine. Such was the power of the *Titanic*'s engines, however, that a terrific suction was set up in the shallow water and both the other liners were dragged from the wharf towards her. The *St Paul* broke adrift and the *Oceanic* was dragged off until a 60 ft gangway dropped from the wharf into the water.

It seemed that a collision was inevitable, in full view of all those who had come to see the *Titanic* off on her maiden, and, as it turned out, her only voyage. At the last moment, with great skill, the *Titanic*'s master, Captain Edward Smith, put his port engine ahead and drove the other vessels back towards the wharf—thus avoiding a nasty pile-up. Tugs standing by swiftly took the vessels under control.

Commander Lightoller, aboard the *Titanic*, recalled the incident vividly in later years. He had sailed many times on the *Oceanic* and, after his miraculous escape from death when he plunged into the icy waters seconds before the *Titanic* slipped below the waves, he returned to the *Oceanic* to be shipwrecked yet again. Several of the seamen survivors from the *Titanic* also moved on to the *Oceanic*.

Lightoller—played by Kenneth More in the highly successful film *A Night to Remember*—wrote his own book, *Titanic And Other Ships*, and told of his adventurous life at sea. Looking back over his career in his old age it was the *Oceanic* rather than the *Titanic* that he remembered as the finest ship he ever sailed in.

Ismay, along with other shipowners, had in previous years negotiated a deal with the Admiralty concerning details in the construction of passenger ships. While the ships were built solely as liners, the Admiralty gave an annual grant towards their upkeep on condition that they could be called in for naval work in the event of war. In addition they were built under certain Admiralty specifications—for example, the *Oceanic* was constructed in such a way that 4·7 inch guns could be mounted very quickly indeed.

So when the *Oceanic* sailed into Southampton just after World War I had begun, she was invaded by a shoal of draughtsmen, naval architects, government representatives and so on. RMS *Oceanic* was to become HMS *Oceanic*, and within a few days the liner was to go off to war as an armed merchant cruiser.

Guns and other equipment were hoisted aboard, including ammunition and stores. The sumptuous fittings on the great liner were left, by and large, as they were—remember, the prevalent feeling at the time was that this 'business with Germany' would be resolved in a few months, and the *Oceanic* would return to her former duties. Ratings and seamen were to enjoy quarters of a grandeur they could never have imagined—the very quarters designed for the millionaires and the star actresses!

Captain Henry Smith had been Master of the *Oceanic* for the two years prior to the war, and had commanded with quiet efficiency. Like many of his officers, he was a member of the Royal Naval Reserve, and along with them and some of the crew he was to stay on the *Oceanic*. Captain William Slayter, of the Royal Navy, was to take charge, with Smith in an undefined advisory capacity, and naval officers and ratings were also to join the ship's company. It is hard to imagine a situation more likely to create a crew split right down the middle.

While the sailors were rapidly put through gun drills, boarding practice and so on, nearly 7,000 tons of coal was stowed in the bunkers—such fuelling today would cost the Royal Navy upwards of £¼ million, while one shudders to think of the wage bill for 600 crew.

Right from the start there appears to have been a marked 'them and us' attitude. Lightoller unwittingly hints at it in his description of the early days under the White Ensign. Describing the merchant seamen on deck before a naval officer for the first time, he writes:

> In response to the order 'those now wishing to remain in the ship, one pace forward, march!', they all quietly walked forward across the deck to make it evident that it was one very good pace. The Navy chap was a bit horrified, but I told him to never mind, they understood in the main what he meant.

Again he pokes gentle fun at the navy's method of putting out a gangway 'by numbers' instead of the usual merchant method which embodied 'the essence of seamanship'.

A rivalry between the two groups of men would be inevitable and perhaps even healthy, but it seems quite possible it became over-intensified. It was this motley mixture that was sent off to the Northern Patrol—with gun crews formed of men who had never seen a gun before, much less fired one. It is hardly surprising that another ship, towing a target for the *Oceanic* gunners to practise on, should send a plaintive suggestion that it was the *target* they should be aiming at!

Among the officers the situation was just as complicated. Many of the senior officers had sailed for some time with Smith, and were used to his orders. Now they had a new Master, which was nothing unusual in itself, but Smith was still on board, though his exact position was unclear. 'No man can serve two Masters'—but the *Oceanic* complement had to try. Furthermore, the two Masters didn't see eye to eye about the methods of running the ship, and the places it would be safe to take her.

On 25 August 1914, the *Oceanic* proudly sailed out of Southampton to war, and started a naval career that was to last no more than a fortnight. Even as she sailed, the crew were still hard at practice with their drills and techniques. Her job was to patrol the difficult waters from the north Scottish mainland to the Faroes, particularly the area around Shetland. She was to stop shipping at her discretion, check their cargoes and personnel, and ensure there were no Germans aboard or indeed any German connection. The marines on board were to carry out the searches.

The *Oceanic* made straight for Scapa Flow in Orkney, Britain's foremost Royal Navy anchorage, with easy access to the North Sea and the Atlantic. She then proceeded north to Shetland, travelling—as she did throughout that fortnight—on a zig-zag course. This was a precaution against submarine attack—a form of warfare considered 'not cricket' by the Admiralty (Churchill, then First Lord, advised pretty savage treatment for captured enemy submarine commanders)—but zig-zagging did call for extremely accurate navigation. In the event it was poor navigation rather than enemy submarines that was to bring about the end of the *Oceanic*.

If the merchantmen thought they were to see some real action in their war, then they would have been disappointed with their spell on the *Oceanic*. They never experienced a wind above Force 4. The ship fired but one shot in anger—across the bows of the inappropriately named SS *Watchful* of Wick—when that ship paid no attention to Captain Slayter's signal to stop. Her wartime booty consisted of a single, terrified German subject found on a Norwegian barque and brought back by the marines in triumph!

Several Shetlanders were members of the *Oceanic*'s crew on that trip and one of them, Johnnie Mann, later recalled how proud he was as she lay at anchor off his home-town port of Lerwick. When he was a small boy in a remote Shetland school, the launch of the famous *Oceanic* had been reported in the newspapers, and had caused such worldwide interest that his schoolteacher had taken the class outside to measure on the road the 704 ft length of the ship.

The small boy, amazed that any ship could be so big, could never have dreamed that one day he would sail on it, and be wrecked on it, and that by the strangest twist of fate all this would happen in his home waters. On 6 September, hundreds of people lined the shore at Lerwick as the *Oceanic* weighed her anchor for what was to be the last time, and steamed off south on the Fair Isle patrol.

Away to the west of the Shetland mainland, on the same latitude as Leningrad and the southernmost tip of Greenland, lies the bleak and spectacular island of Foula, Britain's remotest permanently inhabited community. Lying some 20 miles west of the Shetland mainland, the island was a place to keep well clear of for such a large ship as the *Oceanic*. A far bigger threat was the Hoevdi Grund, or the dreaded Shaalds of Foula—a reef that comes to within a few feet of the surface but which in calm weather gives no warning sign to the unwary. The Shaalds lie just over 2 miles east of Foula, between the island and the Shetland mainland.

We know that the one-time pride of Ismay's fleet got an accurate fix and position west of Foula on the evening of 7 September—bearings were taken on the north and south ends of the island. For historical interest we have tried to trace the various goings-on during that night, and the deeper the delving, the more complicated it becomes. We had to weigh up the evidence, and surmise what actually happened. What is an undeniable fact is that early the following morning, in a flat calm sea and in reasonable visibility, the *Oceanic* was pushed gently but firmly on to the Shaalds by the fast-flowing flood tide and never managed to get off.

The confusion and division between the top command seems to have been almost wholly responsible for the loss. Captain Slayter had taken charge during the night, and early in the following morning had gone below to rest, leaving orders to steer for Foula.

21

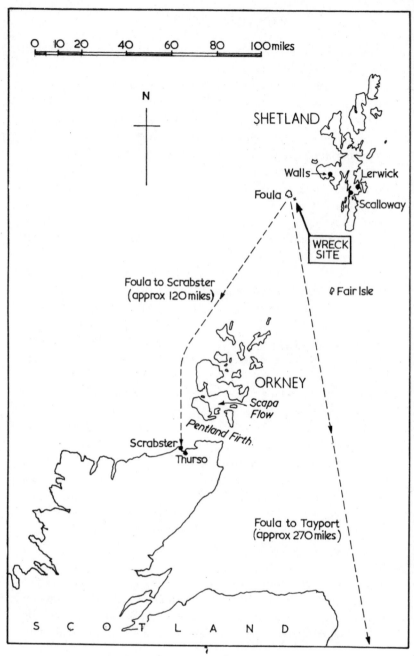

Foula in relation to Shetland, Orkney and the Pentland Firth

Davy Blair, the navigator, had somehow managed to be 13 or 14 miles out in estimating the position of the ship—remember there had been an accurate fix on the land the previous night. But his two superiors had checked his calculations and found nothing untoward. The ship had encountered her first fog of the war, and had stopped engines temporarily: the zig-zagging was obviously confusing her, if not the Germans.

My sketch, omitting the zig-zags, shows roughly what must have happened. Smith, who was only really happy when the ship was in open sea and who had evidently disagreed with Slayter about dodging about the islands, looked at Blair's course and fretted about heading for Foula. 'Turn west', he told young Blair, 'and we'll head out to open sea.'

He thought they were well south of the island, and by going west they would be steering clear of any danger. But they had travelled 14 miles further than they had calculated, and instead of being *south* of Foula they were *east* of it—and east of the Shaalds. So heading west wasn't taking them to open sea, but straight on to the terrible Shaalds. They had no inkling of danger. Even if they were off course, they did not suspect that visibility was much worse than the 7 miles Slayter had estimated before retiring; if that had been the case they would have seen Foula long before reaching the Shaalds.

Everyone on the bridge thought that they were well to the south and west of Foula, and look-outs were instructed to keep a special watch aft on the starboard side, where the island should appear if the morning mist lifted more. There must have been quite a flap when a voice from the crow's nest sang out: 'Land on the starboard bow!' Their calculations were far out.

Another major mistake was made at this point. The golden rule when you suddenly find yourself somewhere you shouldn't be at sea is to go astern on a reciprocal course—in other words, go backwards the way you came in. If you didn't hit anything coming in, then you won't hit anything going out. But Smith reckoned that Foula was 4 or 5 miles off—so he was sure he was nowhere near the Shaalds—and in any case he still suspected

WHY 'THE OTHER TITANIC'?

they were to the south of the isle. As a result, he ordered light starboarding.

Even allowing for the errors in position, he might just have got away with it by the greatest of good fortune. It appears that he would have come south of the Shaalds, turned north through the narrow gap of deep water between the reef and Foula, and escaped by the skin of his teeth.

There then came about a classic 'too many cooks spoil the broth' situation. Slayter arrived on deck at this moment, made a quick and incorrect appreciation of the position, and countermanded the orders. He shouted to Blair to take a fix on the land which was becoming clearer by the minute, and pinpoint their exact position. The ship was put hard-astarboard, and Blair returned after carrying out the most accurate piece of navigating for some time. 'We're close to the Hoevdi Reef,' he cried, and almost as he spoke the ship touched lightly aft and took the ground forward. The fast-flowing flood tide was pushing her firmly on to the reef.

Unlike such great liners as the *Titanic* and the *Lusitania*, the *Oceanic*'s end was not marked by any loss of life. She sat statuesquely on the reef, almost as if she were in dry dock. Soon the Aberdeen trawler *Glenogil* came close to the wreck and tried to tow the *Oceanic*'s stern off the reef. Such was the strength of the tide that the *Glenogil* herself would have made only slow progress, and she had absolutely no chance of doing anything for the massive ship, now lolling like a stranded whale. Other naval ships in the area were called to try to give assistance, and men were flitted by lifeboat to the *Glenogil*, which in turn took them out to the other ships standing by, the *Alsatian* and the *Forward*.

At 4.30 that afternoon the *Forward* tried to tow the *Oceanic* off, and a heavy towing hawser was prepared on the stranded ship. A Foula eyewitness wrote: 'The cruiser came from the north at a great speed. She slowed down on approaching the liner, and it was a lesson in caution to see her sounding and measuring every inch of the sea.'

24

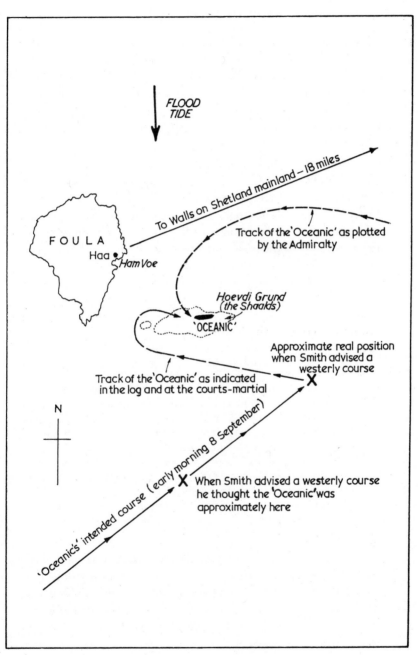

Oceanic's tracks, notional and actual

The end of a 9 in hawser was got to the *Forward*, and the now north-ebbing tide would assist in the salvage attempt. As the slack was taken up, the hawser held for a moment, went rigid as the *Oceanic* held fast, and then snapped as easily as a piece of wool. The *Oceanic* was now listing markedly, and an inspection showed that, as a result of the heavy bumping, three of her holds were full of water. The boiler fires had long since been extinguished, and the salvage men realised that even if they could pull the ship off, they were so far from any shelter or repair facilities that she would certainly sink.

Within twenty-four hours of her striking, the whole ship's company had been safely taken off. The weather, considering the month was September and the place Foula, was still very good. Lightoller wrote about the wreck years later, and his tale certainly improved with age—he described the ship running aground in a 'huge sea' and being 'pounded to pieces'. On any ship running on to the Shaalds in such conditions there would have been a considerable loss of life.

He went on:

> Lying broadside on to the reef, with the tide setting strong on to it, she was held there, lifting and falling each time with a horrible grinding crash, I know it nearly broke my heart to feel her going to bits under my very feet, after all these years. The sensation, as those knife-edged rocks ground and crunched their way through her bilge plates, was physically sickening. How she held together for us to get everyone out of her was a miracle in itself, and certainly testified to the good work put in by Harland and Wolff. We had our work cut out to get the stokers and engineers away without loss of life.

The 573-ton Admiralty salvage vessel *Lyons* was sent north to see whether it was possible to save the ship. Using hindsight and our knowledge of the reef and its tides, it was obvious that the *Oceanic* was to all intents and purposes a write-off the moment she struck. But Lieutenant Gardiner of the *Lyons* initially had great hopes that she could be salved, and it was a great blow when he was ordered not to try for the ship, but to concentrate on recovering the guns, as much ammunition as possible, and the stores. All the guns and all except one of the gunshields were recovered.

Twenty-two Foula men were signed on to assist in this work, and day after day in that most unusual Indian summer Shetland was enjoying, they made their way out to the wreck to help with the recoveries. Peter Gray of Burns, who died while we were on Foula, told us of the excitement of going out to the *Oceanic* to help recover as much as possible. He recalled looking down into the massive engine-room, with the sea swirling in and out.

Islanders everywhere reckon that a wreck is fair game—a policy not recognised by the gentlemen of Her Majesty's Customs and Excise Department—and Foula men certainly are no different. Tales exist from Cornwall to Kirkwall of local ministers praying for a safe passage for those at sea 'though, Lord, if there must be a wreck, let it be on our shores.'

The Foula folk still recall how their men returned from the stranded wreck with their pockets bulging and jingling with small fittings they had smuggled off the ship. Those in charge of the salvage work would have turned a blind eye to this, particularly as the ship had been written off anyway.

Another Foula man told the tale of their final day on the *Oceanic*. Some of the men had found where the ship's silverware was kept, and this too had been abandoned. They could only take as much as would fit into their pockets and at the very last moment, just when they were about to leave the ship, someone stumbled over the tobacco bond. To the Foula men there was no choice. Much to the annoyance of the womenfolk back on the isle, the knives and forks were thrown back into the ship, and it was the tobacco that was stuffed into the pockets. 'We soon smoked it,' he recalled, 'and then we had nothing to show for it. I don't think the women understood, or forgave us for a while!'

But not all the fittings were abandoned for pocketsful of

tobacco. To this day you might sit down to tea in a Foula household, enjoying the marvellous hospitality of the island folk, and if you look closely at the spotless white tablecloth, and the steaming pot of tea by the side of your hostess, you might just notice that they both carry the motif of one of the world's most famous shipping lines—the White Star flag.

Commander Smith is said to have come ashore at Foula's tiny pier, looked out to sea at his stranded ship 2 miles off, and commented that the ship would stay on the reef as a monument and nothing would move it. One of the Foula men, knowing the full fury and power of a Shetland storm, muttered: 'I'll give her two weeks.'

On Sunday, 29 September a gale arose from the north-west, and all day heavy seas swept over the deck of the former liner. Bobby Isbister, just fifteen years old at the time, recalls it well, and marvelled at the battle between the sea and the proud ship. 'I remember seeing her mast come crashing down,' he told me. 'The next day I looked out to sea and she had disappeared.'

Folk always talked of her slipping off the reef and sinking in deeper water. Professor Ian Holbourn, owner of Foula at the time and author of a book on the isle, wrote: 'Before long a gale blew up and the great ship slipped below the waves. We often think longingly of the many tons of coal, blankets, linen, pianos, and all the furniture of the luxury liner lying just beyond our reach, so near and yet so far.'

Slipped off into deeper water? This seems to offer the only explanation why such a vast bulk of ship could be sitting well clear of the water one night and completely out of sight the next day. But it did not happen that way. Thirty thousand tons of steel, constructed as one of the world's finest ships and sitting marooned in 30 ft of water, collapsed like a house of cards and became 30,000 tons of scrap wreckage overnight. It was as if she were completely dismantled and broken up in a shipbreaker's yard. Sides of the ship, decks, funnels would all have groaned, cracked, crumbled and been spectacularly torn into pieces by the fury of a single Shetland gale.

When the weather had worsened, Gardiner had had to scuttle to Scalloway for shelter, and from the safe anchorage he wrote to his rear-admiral that the Admiralty charts showing the Hoevdi Ground were not accurate, though this in no way contributed to the wrecking. The reef was so shallow at one point, he claimed, that a Foula fisherman had wanted to get out of his boat at a very low water, just so he could boast to his friends that he had actually stood on the Hoevdi. He reckoned his head would just stick out of the water!

When Gardiner learned that the ship had finally broken up, he made his way south. The Admiralty, who had taken over the ship's responsibilities at the outbreak of the war, paid out compensation to the White Star Line. The *Oceanic*, as far as they were concerned, had had an inglorious war and was a total loss.

The episode was not over for Slayter, Smith and Blair, and each man went south to face a court martial. The full details of these are still not available to the public, but I did trace a report on the proceedings in the *Naval and Military Record*, the Ship's Log, and eye-witness reports from Foula and the Shetland mainland. To me, these show, quite clearly, evasiveness, deception, manifest incompetence and an appalling muddle—and the court-martial findings have all the hallmarks of a 'whitewash' operation by the Admiralty. Incredibly both Slayter and Smith got off completely free, while Blair was reprimanded on a technicality.

Traditionally, certainly in those times, the captain of a ship normally took full responsibility for any disaster, whatever the circumstances. This was not the case with the *Oceanic*. Slayter was to point out what was certainly a very unusual situation. Aboard the *Oceanic* was the old Master, surrounded by many of his old officers, a man who was in charge of the bridge for the last few hours of the *Oceanic*'s journey. Slayter said that he took charge of the ship at night, while Smith was in charge during the day when he, Slayter, was resting.

Smith did not try to defend his various actions on the bridge of the *Oceanic*, but rather argued his case, successfully, on a

29

technicality. He told the court he was acting commander, but that he had received no orders, either written or oral, to carry out duties on the *Oceanic*, and therefore could not take the ultimate responsibility. It is no secret that he disagreed strongly that the *Oceanic* should be taken into such awkward positions, but he was obeying Slayter's instructions. Thus when things went wrong, he was not prepared to accept the ultimate responsibility. Despite all his experience he found himself 'a glorified look-out man'.

The masters of two Cunard liners, on hearing about the case, took the side of their merchant colleague and were reported as saying: 'Smith told the naval captain that it was too dangerous, in a fog, to take a ship the size of the *Oceanic* where the latter suggested. The naval captain told Smith he was only a merchant ship master, and no longer in command of the ship, and that she would go where he, the naval captain, said she would go. And go there she did—on to the reef, breaking her back.'

Without the benefit of the full court-martial reports we can't yet know exactly what happened, but obviously the split between the two men—and the sheer folly of the loss—was very apparent in shipping circles at the time.

Blair was the only one to receive any sort of censure. He would have been less than human if he did not feel he had been used as a scapegoat. He was condemned for not sounding, and 'reprimanded'. Yet he had suggested sounding to Commander Smith, only to be told—wrongly—that as they were south of Foula this would serve no purpose. He was also found guilty of not ordering the ship to be stopped as soon as land was sighted in an unexpected position, but Smith obviously, in reality if not officially, was very much the man in charge. Blair must have been a very disillusioned young man when he was found guilty, and even more so when he was to see his two superiors walk away without blemish on their names.

We have a copy of the Ship's Log, which covered her entire naval career. Each page is concisely and neatly written up—with the exception of the page covering the last few hours! There we get splodges, alterations (is that a '1' turned into a '3' or a '3' turned into a '1'?) and even the classic schoolboy dodge on the entry for the critical time for the final change of course—a small puddle of ink obliterating everything. One does not need to be over-cynical to suspect that there was some cooking of the books!

Of course we must accept the fact that when your ship runs aground you have many more important things to think about than merely keeping a neat log, but there do seem to be many suspicious alterations. Perhaps the alterations were made later, purely to show what actually happened, but there remains the suspicion that it was an attempt to explain away the disaster. If everything happened as recorded, the *Oceanic* would have sailed majestically past the south end of Foula on that sunlit morning, making her way west to open sea—perhaps to some other war disaster. Who knows?

In theory alterations on the Ship's Log could easily be checked against the Engine-Room Log. But Slayter explained to the court that this had been kept in the mercantile marine method—on scraps of paper—and these had been lost. The chance of embarrassing comparison was gone.

There was total confusion on the ship over time. The *Oceanic* would have been most vulnerable to submarine attack just around daylight, so the ship's company went on general alert before daybreak and remained so until daylight was established. This was deemed to be hard on the men of the middle watch, who had already been at their guns for a whole watch, and then had to turn out again a few minutes after they had gone below. Slayter authorised the clock to be put back forty minutes, so that the watch and alert could be merged into one.

The simplest way would surely have been to keep all the clocks at the same time, and alter the times that the watches had to turn out. Under the system adopted everyone seemed to get hopelessly muddled, and it's very possible this contributed directly to the loss. Slayter himself was to confess: 'The officers were directed to write up the Log in Routine Time (i.e. the altered times) and when the navigator wrote the Fair Log he would make the necessary corrections to bring it to **GMT**. The officers did not seem to have quite understood the change, and various discrepancies arose.' A recipe for utter confusion!

It also seems very possible that during the night calculations as to the position of the *Oceanic* were made using time figures which were partly Routine Time and partly GMT. If this were the case—and Slayter himself hints that it might have been—then this could explain how the former liner was 13 or 14 miles out in dead reckoning, only 12 hours after taking an accurate land fix. Blair said that at the moment they struck, his paper calculations estimated the ship to be 13 or 14 miles south-west of where she actually was.

The errors didn't stop there. Slayter was questioned about discrepancies between the Ship's Log and an engine-room register—these were the result of a 'clerical error' he said, in a surprisingly lame excuse which, even more surprisingly, according to the reports we have, was not followed up by another question from the prosecution. Even when they found themselves in such a dangerous position they should still have been able to escape, because by good fortune the early morning mist pulled clear in time to show Foula stretched out like a mural in front of them. Both Smith and Slayter thought they were some 5 miles off the island—in fact they were scarcely more than 2! It seems astonishing that not one, but two, very experienced seamen should make the same mistake.

The *Oceanic* crew were jokingly referred to by other members of the Fleet as the 'Muckle Flugga Hussars'—Muckle Flugga is the most northerly point of the British Isles, and the jest was that the crew might be best on horseback! Certainly the performance on the bridge that morning of 8 September suggests they would have been safer on dry land.

Another very unusual piece of evidence we were to find in the archives was an Admiralty chart marking the position of the wreck on the reef. It looks like an entry for a newspaper 'Spot the Ball' football competition, with *Oceanics* rather than crosses liberally scattered about. In blue there is the position as plotted

1 The *Oceanic* in her prime (*Harland & Wolff, Belfast*)

2 A heavily appointed stateroom on board (*Harland & Wolff, Belfast*)

by her officers after the grounding, but it was noted that one bearing was wrongly calculated. A green *Oceanic*, worked out later by navigational experts, plotted the same bearings correctly.

Another naval ship on the scene plotted a black *Oceanic*, perched far higher on the reef than she could possibly have reached in such fine weather conditions. Finally Lt Gardiner plots a red *Oceanic*, further to the east, and by the look of the chart if she had stayed in that same position since 1914 she would still be afloat! If I had to judge this 'Spot the Wreck' competition I would give it to 'green' as the nearest miss.

It is hard to believe that with the *Oceanic* hard on the rocks, and Foula laid out on their port side—with all the details before them, and all day to work out their position—mistakes were still made. When they failed to take accurate bearings even in that situation, then surely we can doubt the accuracy of anything they say.

Most amazing of all, however, must be the charted track of the *Oceanic* produced in a sketch at the courts martial. It fits exactly with the description made in the press by a Foula eye-witness at the time: 'The ship was coming from the north. If she had kept going south she would have been all right but she turned east.' On the chart a line is marked showing a gradual *port* turn until she went on the reef. In the prevailing conditions it is the most logical way for the ship to get to her final stranded position. Yet *all* the oral evidence makes it clear that the ship was coming from the south, was starboarded, and the plotted port turn on this chart was never mentioned.

Looking at all the evidence—the courts martial, the Ship's Log, contemporary reports and our own knowledge of the reef and the waters surrounding it—I can come to only one conclusion as to the loss of the *Oceanic*. For some reason their Lordships at the Admiralty decided to do a 'whitewash job' on Slayter and Smith. They would issue only a minor reprimand to Blair. There can be no other possibility when a naval ship, functioning perfectly and under no enemy duress, sights land while proceeding in perfect sea conditions, and runs forward on to a charted reef—and her captain is then exonerated and has his sword returned to him by the president of the court martial 'with the greatest possible pleasure'.

Why? The only explanation I could arrive at lies in the fact that war had only just begun. The navy had taken over what was still a world-famous ship—the Queen of the Seas. Within a fortnight of her leaving on her first mission she was incompetently parked on a lonely reef in what must have been one of the least glorious moments in Britain's famous naval history. To reveal such incompetence at such an early stage of the war would have done nothing for naval and national morale. A whitewash would avoid all that.

The *Oceanic* was to remain just a name for the records until a light flurry in the 1920s. The Admiralty began circulating private firms with a view to having salvage work carried out in Scapa Flow on the captured German fleet, which had been deliberately and spectacularly scuttled by the Germans in 1919. It is interesting that the Admiralty's own salvage methods and skills were far behind those of the top private concerns, and while they touted for tenders for the Scapa job they also circulated details of the *Oceanic*. Enquiries came in from such well-known scrap firms as George Cohen & Sons, who wanted to know if the wreck was high and dry at low water, and dropped the subject fast when they heard it wasn't. The North-East Salvage and Shipbreaking Co asked for the exact position of the wreck, were given it, and also promptly forgot the project when they pinpointed the spot on their charts.

The Scapa Flow Salvage and Shipbreaking Co Ltd was formed in June 1923 and was the first firm to work on the scuttled fleet. Though it was Cox & Danks (later Metal Industries) who were later to carry out some truly incredible salvage feats in Scapa, it was the Shetland-based Scapa Flow company that first worked there. Headed by the former Shetland county convenor, J.W. Robertson, with his brother Robbie as chief diver, the group had ambitious salvage plans. They paid the Admiralty £400 for four of the scuttled German destroyers, and though they were partly successful in this venture, they soon ran into problems with the Admiralty over the hire of some suitable equipment.

Expenses were high and profits low, so 'J.W.' looked for something nearer home. He became interested in the *Oceanic* and offered the Department of Contracts a mere £50 for the whole wreck. The department checked with the Hydrographer and received a terse reply:

> The sum offered in effect amounts to nothing more than a gift, and lays down a dangerous precedent in this respect. Mr Robertson is fully aware of the conditions prevailing, and appears to wish to acquire everything under the sea in the Orkneys and Shetlands. If he does not make greater headway in this venture than he is making in his attempts at Scapa, not much progress or benefit is likely to result. We know he possesses no plant. As a matter of Admiralty policy, and the undesirability of establishing any such precedent, it is recommended that Mr Robertson's offer be declined.

Because of the very wild spot where the *Oceanic*'s remains lay, the Admiralty refused to consider hiring him any equipment for the job, and indicated that they would only sell their rights in the wreck 'for a substantial sum'. J.W. travelled to London and made an oral request for an eight-week option to buy the wreck for £200.

This request for an option seemed to baffle the Admiralty, who wondered what J.W. might be getting up to, but eventually they decided to accept his offer, giving him his eight weeks' grace.

Shrewdly J.W. wanted to have a look at the *Oceanic* before committing £200 to the project. But he was held up in his Scapa Flow operations, and fell out with the Admiralty over the hire of the equipment. He had to write to ask for an extension to the eight weeks, and complained of the lack of Admiralty support. The Admiralty let him have his extension, but scolded him in their reply:

Regarding your remarks as to the alleged delay in supplying your firm with salvage craft for raising the ex-German destroyers, the Admiralty must again call your attention to the fact that no delay should have occurred in the lifting craft being taken over by you had you agreed to the usual Admiralty terms for hire of such craft, as communicated to you when you approached the Admiralty.

With relations strained and their salvage work in the Flow held up, the second extension on the *Oceanic* ran out. The Robertsons had to make a decision quickly, and they had to make it blind without visiting the *Oceanic* site. So £200 they could ill afford was paid to the Admiralty, and they became the new owners of the *Oceanic*.

It was in the summer of 1924 that Robbie and his second diver made the trip to Foula to inspect the wreck. Their heavy equipment was ferried up to Walls, a small, remote village and sheltered anchorage on the west side of the Shetland mainland. There they were met by the Foula mail boat which had made the crossing for stores and supplies. The diving dress, the lead boots, the brass helmets and the pump were all carefully stowed aboard before the tough island seamen, with a mixture of oars and sail, pulled their way out of the sheltered waters across the wild 18-mile, open-sea stretch to Foula.

Foula has no sheltered harbour, so at the end of their trip the mail boat had to be unloaded and pulled up a small stretch of sand at Ham Voe. Robbie is still widely remembered on Shetland for his ability to tell a tale—or perhaps I should say a tall tale—and we can be sure that many a yarn was told on the trip and around the croft-house fire at Ham that evening.

But he must have been nervous of the work that lay ahead of him the next day. The Foula folk knew the Shaalds well, for they provided some of the best fishing they had. The fast-flowing waters provided plentiful feed for the piltock, and at times the islanders hauled them out on their handlines almost non-stop. So famous had it become that there was a special song about the reef—the Shaalds of Foula—in which they sing 'The Shaalds will pey for it aa', boys' (roughly translated as 'We'll make our

38

living on the Shaalds'). There is also a dance to the tune, and to this day it is usually the first dance at a Foula celebration.

The reef was also infamous. When tides move in deep open water, there is an unrestricted flow and the water moves at a slow speed. If a large volume of water is suddenly required to move over a shallow reef, then the water is pushed through much faster. Throw in the complexities of the meeting of the North Sea and the Atlantic not far off, and the solid rock that is Foula just 2 miles away, and you have the makings of a very nasty tide-race—the Shaalds. If the tide turned against the wind, for example, pleasant sea conditions could be turned into a heaving, bucking and confused maelstrom in minutes.

So Robbie checked his gear with extra care the following morning as the islanders heaved at the oars on the trip out to the reef. They all had vivid memories of the liner on the reef ten years before, and could take Robbie directly to the spot where they last saw her. The anchor was sent spinning over the side, and it was with considerable apprehension that Robbie saw the tide whistling past the boat. Still, £200 had been spent, and they had to get on with it.

As he was lowered over the side, the tide caught hold of his body and pulled him well to the stern of the boat. There was much anxiety on top, but soon the faint signal indicating he had reached the bottom was received on the surface. He didn't seem to be moving, and moments later the urgent signal to haul him up quickly was given.

Working furiously, the men hauled a very distressed diver to the surface. Robbie was completely exhausted and it was with considerable difficulty they pulled him aboard, such was the grip of the tide. What he actually saw we will never know, for the reports of the dive became more exaggerated each time he told the tale.

Andrew Umphrey, a crofter at Leraback who also died while we were at Foula, was a crew member that day. 'Robbie was so exhausted that for some time he was unable to speak. He later said he spent most of his time hiding behind a rock from the worst of the tide, and that he wouldn't go down there again for a king's ransom. The diver who was with him absolutely refused to go in after seeing Robbie's plight.'

The company's bold and expensive venture had failed almost before it had started, and that day a myth was created. His diving tall stories are still legendary on the islands—of how a distraught Admiral Lord Jellicoe supposedly greeted Diver Robertson in Scapa Flow during World War I with the words 'Ah! Robertson. Thank God you're here! The Germans have left port and I don't know what to do'; of lobsters crawling up to him and tapping his visor with their claws out of sheer curiosity; or of how he navigated a salvage vessel from Lerwick to Scapa Flow in a fog so thick that he couldn't see his outstretched hand in front of him, but nonetheless managed to throw the anchor right down the funnel of the German destroyer they had come to work on. The tales are endless.

Robbie was a diver with many achievements in pier work which he could justifiably be proud of, but whose salvage successes seemed to be most numerous when standing at a bar with a merry crowd of awe-struck listeners alongside. He is not unique in that, and indeed the breed flourishes today. The 'undiveable *Oceanic*' became the accepted tale, and while few believed many of Robbie's wilder exaggerations, the core of his story was believed. How else could such an incredibly rich ship, in terms of fittings, remain totally undisturbed as the decades went by, including the 1960s when the sport of aqualung diving really took off, and even into the 70s? We don't even know for sure that Robbie got on to the wreck site in his abortive dive, but certainly no one followed him. Not so much as a single scrap of metal was taken from the wreck.

The Scapa Flow company was not to prosper. Although they did make some successful lifts in the Flow they were not to make the fortune that J.W., the supreme optimist (most salvage operators are!), had predicted. In 1927 they changed their name to Robertson (Lerwick) Ltd, and the diving and salvage side of the business was run down. Both J.W. and Robbie had been dead for some years, and the company little more than a name when it was taken over in 1969 by a prominent and long-established Shetland concern Hay & Company (Lerwick) Ltd. Among the assets transferred that day, unknown to or forgotten by both parties, were the remains of the once biggest and finest ship in the world.

2

The *Oceanic* After Sixty Years

Most of this history, however, was quite unknown to us in the summer of 1973, as Alec Crawford and I enjoyed carefree diving on Fair Isle, that lovely little island set midway between the Orkneys and the Shetlands. For once we weren't looking for financial return; we'd had a hard winter's work, diving for clams, and we'd decided to take the summer off to return to Fair Isle, an island of which we both had happy memories. By August we were beginning to prepare for our return to the mainland—we certainly had no thoughts of visiting Foula, that wild outcrop of rock we could see on clear days, jutting against the sky 50 miles away to the north-west.

So our trip to Foula was pure chance. Fair Isle has a world-famous bird observatory, and at this time a group of ornithologists just happened to plan a day's visit to Foula, where there is spectacular and much less 'watched' bird life. They would charter Loganair's Islander aircraft from Sumburgh some 20 miles to the north on the Shetland mainland, fly across to Foula to spend a few hours there, and be returned to Fair Isle that evening. However, they had one seat spare on the plane. Would one of us like to take the £10 seat?

We began to review the little we knew about the *Oceanic*. The fishermen all said diving would be crazy, if not impossible. But could they, possibly, be just a little bit pessimistic? That day Alec was no bird-watcher or day-tripper. While his fellow travellers were taking to the hills to view the bonxies and skuas, Alec sought out Bobby Isbister, born the year the *Oceanic* was built and a lad of fifteen when the great ship wallowed on the reef. He had been to sea himself as a young man, and knew what he was talking about. He was full of tales of wrecks around the island, but concerning the reef his warning was short and to the point. 'Don't dive on the Shaalds!'

Bobby pointed to the south end of the isle, a few hundred yards from his own croft. There, in 1899, a North Shields line-fishing boat drove on to the rocks at night in a blizzard. There were no survivors. Next he pointed to the north and east, and outlined the tale of a schooner that went ashore there after World War II. There might be pickings there. Alec moved north and was favourably impressed with the pier at Ham Voe. It was ideal for our inflatable boat, though nothing bigger, and was sheltered from all but heavy weather from the east. And finally he met Elizabeth Holbourn, who was to become our closest neighbour for six years and a good friend. Yes, she would have a word with the island trustees and we might be able to stay in their house just above the pier for a week or so.

Foula was then, and still is now, a complete contrast to Fair Isle. Foula looks much more like the typical, traditional, isolated island. Unlike Fair Isle, most of the homes had no running water, and no electricity. The Foula croft houses were much simpler, but in their way very attractive. It was obvious at a glance that Foula had not enjoyed the investment in improvements of the modern Fair Isle. Yet Fair Isle had almost been evacuated in the 1950s, while bleaker Foula had kept a constant though tiny population with no talk of evacuation.

Alec returned wildly enthusiastic, and we soon decided that we would go to Foula to dive. The Fair Isle mail boat agreed to run us to Foula for a moderate fee. We planned to have a dive on the two coastal wrecks Bobby Isbister had told us about, and thought we would make sufficient recoveries to pay for the boat hire. At the same time we started to dream of the 'undiveable shipwreck'.

The seemingly insurmountable problem was the strength of the tide. Writing about the wrecking in his book on Foula, Professor Holbourn noted:

The launch of the *Lyons*, a salvage boat which hurried to the scene, was capable of a speed of ten knots, yet was unable to make any headway against the tide although she tried for 15 minutes. Even then it was not the top of the tide, and the officer in charge reckoned the full tide would be 12 knots. He confessed he would not have believed it had he been told.

A 12 knot tide? Robbie's estimates, passed down by word of mouth, calculated it as even faster than that at its peak flow. Many a sport diver has made wild claims about tidal speeds he has dived in, but you can take it from me that if a diver is working in a 2 knot tide he's got plenty of problems, and in much over that he can't continue. So the 12 knots claim really made us consider that diving on the Shaalds might indeed be impossible. (In fact, with the years of experience we gained on the reef, and from the knowledge of local fishermen, we estimated a peak flow on the Shaalds of around 6 knots—as a result we had to do all our work in the short, slackish periods around the turn of the tide.)

But we would go to Foula to see for ourselves.

The arrival of our salvage equipment and personnel at Foula's tiny, awkwardly placed pier was hardly an impressive sight. Our equipment in the hold of the Fair Isle mail boat, *Good Shepherd III*, seemed hardly sufficient for a good weekend's diving—certainly it was a humble prelude to what was to be a major salvage job. We were travelling light, for we did not expect to stay long and had no idea how we would get back to Fair Isle.

Off came the multi-patched inflatable with an outboard engine that had seen service in Southern Ireland six years earlier—in fact it wasn't new even then. Next were three twin aqualung sets and two demand valves, with other basic diving gear. A few assorted tools, including a sledgehammer and axe which could be used in a primitive way to break up scrap metal on shore, were followed by our 'lifting equipment'—12 fathoms of light polypropylene rope! 'You'll soon have the *Oceanic* apart with that,' jested a fisherman on the pier, indicating the tools. Personal gear, if I remember rightly, consisted of what we stood up in and a clean shirt between the two of us.

As our stay was only to be a short one, the Holbourn family generously allowed us to live in the Haa (Shetland dialect for Hall) above the pier. Foula had been bought by Professor Holbourn at the turn of the century and, while his two surviving sons did not live on the isle, they were frequent visitors to it, and the Haa, though empty for most of the year, was a family base. Four of the professor's grandchildren, however, make Foula their permanent home.

We arrived on 22 August 1973, and our good fortune extended to fine weather conditions. Later experience was to show that the end of August was usually the time to be packing up for the year, rather than starting operations, since September and the equinox can bring the fiercest gales of the year. But this year we were able to dive until October before the storms—both natural and in the court room—were to drive us from the reef.

At this stage we played our *Oceanic* aspirations in a very low key, genuinely believing that the two coastal wrecks we had heard about, the 'fishing boat *Teal Duck* and the schooner *Nordsternen*, would provide the metal to pay for our short trip. We had not discussed, even between ourselves, the possibility of any salvage work on the *Oceanic*, though on our arrival at Foula we went ahead with plans to locate the former White Star liner. At that time we knew virtually nothing about the history of the ship and its wrecking, but the islanders told us she had stood majestically on the reef for a fortnight. One night, they said, she was towering out of the sea, and the next morning she was gone. To disappear as quickly as she had done, we reckoned that she would have to be lying in at least ten fathoms of water.

Whenever we arrive to dive on a new location, we always make straight for the local fishermen to check positions, tides, obstructions, dangers and so on. This was particularly the case on Foula, because of the dangerous reputation of the Shaalds that we already knew much about. We were both reasonably experienced divers who knew what we could and could not do, but constant 'doom and disaster' warnings, given with very real concern for our welfare, sowed seeds of doubt in our minds. Would we end up like Robbie after his dive—or worse?

Still, we reasoned, Robbie had been diving in the old hard hat gear, with his air and communication lines running to the surface. These would catch the tide in flow, and he would be dragged all over the place. We had the modern self-contained underwater breathing apparatus (SCUBA) gear, and dived free. We had no contact with the surface and no line attached to us. The diver would be completely on his own and entirely responsible for himself. But—unlike Robbie—he had great freedom of movement in his equipment, and no lines to cause extra tidal drag.

The following day we prepared our boat at the pier, and carefully stowed and checked our gear. We tried to look calm and nonchalant in front of the well wishers who had come to see us off—still issuing many a dire warning. The problems of Robbie's dip half a century before came flooding back to us time and time again. We could almost read in the faces of some of those on the pier the thought: 'Are they going to come back in one piece?'

Armed with the Admiralty chart which marked both reef and the wreck, we made our way out to the Shaalds. We had checked carefully with local lobstermen when we would get slackish water on the reef—such was the confusion of the tidal pattern on the Shaalds that it was midwater at the pier (just 2 miles from the reef) when it was slack on the reef itself. We scarcely believed it at first, but it was true.

We marked off our anchor line at 2 fathom intervals so that we could estimate our depth. It was no easy matter, at more than 2 miles distance, to line up the features on the chart with features visible to the eye while being thrown about like something in a washing machine (a common experience in an inflatable on a choppy reef!). If depths of more than 10 fathoms of water were sounded, we tried another spot.

Time after time Alec manoeuvred the inflatable into position, taking close note of the behaviour of the tide. When he had picked his spot—by calculation from the chart and from the visual marks on the island—he would shout 'Now!' and I would hurl the anchor as far uptide as I could. Often the flow of the tide would pull the anchor jerkily across the bottom and we would drift. Then, catching a particular crevice, it would come fast.

Each time this happened I would pull twin aqualung cylinders on to my back, adjust my face mask, push the single hose demand valve into my mouth, and roll over the side of the boat hanging on to the rope running down the outside of the pontoon. I would then drag myself forward to the anchor rope and inch my way to the bottom—with water flashing past me like a river in spate—almost like climbing a rope in reverse. Eyes straining into the opaque greenness, I would often pick out shapes which at first looked like wreckage, but on closer inspection would turn out to be nothing more than gigantic boulders which must have been rolled off the reef countless thousands of years ago. Reaching the bottom, often slightly distressed because of the forces of surge and tide, I would pause for a moment, get myself sorted out, and pick up the anchor in my arms.

Then I was off on an effortless 'swim'. Both man and boat were wholly under the spell of the tide—I didn't have to use my fins at all. Like a twig in a river I was swept along, looking all around me for some tiny piece of steel wreckage, just something to show we were near the wreck. I wasn't even sure what I was looking for—just a tiny clue or something man-made that would shout out in this incredible environment. I remember feeling disappointment and impatience as we continued to draw blanks, but looking back on it my heart was thumping with excitement and anticipation. I was thrilled to be on this magnificent unexplored reef miles out to sea from a picture-book island.

Floating with me, governed by that same tide, were shoals of piltock drawn into the reef by the feed provided on the fast-flowing and ebbing tides. The vast boulders provided perfect citadels for scores of heavily armoured crabs and lobsters, claws out, ready to repel or attack. In the shallower water, thick kelp streamed out like palm trees in a hurricane, only their size and the steely grip of their roots holding the stalks in position. People might expect a professional diver to be blasé in such circumstances, but I vividly recall drinking in the splendour of it all. But we were there for a job, and I would willingly have swapped it all for just one scrap of steel to tell us we were near our goal.

After I had tumbled perhaps 800 yd down the reef in the grip of the tide, I would surface, finning hard to push myself up through the stream, still holding the anchor. Quickly Alec would gather in the slack, and I would be hanging on the side of the boat, still wearing the twin aqualung and a lead-weight belt—the total coming to well over ½ cwt. Because of the buoyancy of my 6·5 mm diving suit I managed to keep myself on the surface without too much difficulty, but the tide tore at my legs and body which streamed out until I was practically lying on the surface. I could do no more than hang on in such tide—and even that was a struggle—until Alec leaned over, grasped the manifold that joined my two cylinders, and hauled the floundering body, gasping like a landed fish, into the bottom of the boat.

Then, as we drifted off south in the flood tide, Alec would interrogate me. 'Did you see any clues? Anything unnatural? Even an anchor or chain?' I would shake my head and he would yank the pull start on the Evinrude outboard engine, push it into gear, and nose north to pick a new spot to try. Time and again we tried unsuccessfully, until the ever-accelerating tide became too much for us. Slightly dispirited and very disappointed at the day's results we made our way back to the Ham.

However, our day was not totally without success. Even though we had our problems, with our modern equipment we had managed far better than Robbie had and, unlike him, were quite prepared to come back for more. In addition our efforts had been closely watched through powerful glasses by some of the islanders, including Harry Gear, the postmaster. He feared we could get ourselves into real trouble and though we had failed to produce a single piece of wreckage we had at least demonstrated that we could dive on the Shaalds, though hardly with ease.

When it was obvious to the islanders that we were not on a complete fool's errand, the mail-boat skipper quickly offered to help us. Six and a half feet tall, massively built and with the legendary strength of the old Foula men, Jim Gear is only dwarfed by his big brother, Ken! In addition to skippering the island's small and sometimes temperamental mail boat, he had a wealth of experience of the waters around Foula from his fishing and lobstering activities. Much of the fish he used for bait was caught on the Shaalds.

Jim was in his thirties, so the *Oceanic* had been wrecked many years before he was born. But many a time he had fished the Shaalds with his late father, Davy, also a mail-boat skipper. Davy had seen the *Oceanic* on the reef, and had often pointed out to his youngest son exactly where she had lain. It was of no direct consequence to them, except when they were fishing in the area, because then hooks dropped close to the wreck site used to hold fast and be lost. He volunteered to take us to the spot his father had pointed out.

With the help of the local tide tables and his interpretation of the conditions, Jim helped us plot the time we could expect the slackest water. For the second successive day we prepared our inflatable, loaded our equipment, recharged aqualungs, and stowed our ropes. Jim took his own beautifully maintained Shetland-built open boat, *Happy Voyager*, powered by an inboard engine. He knew the marks or, as they call them in Shetland, the medes of the *Oceanic*. Let me explain how they work.

If a fisherman is in a certain spot way out to sea and wants to return to the same position at a later date without using sophisticated navigational instruments, he will line up points at the north and south ends of the island. Looking north he will line up a particular rock he knows, perhaps with a scar from a peat bank. To the south he will note that the north gable-end of a house and the edge of a cliff face are in the line. He will remember these and if he lines both up at a later date he must be in the same spot as before. He will even be able to tell another islander where the medes are—usually where fish have been plentiful—and the second man will be able to go to the same spot.

Medes are passed down from generation to generation, and as a young boy Jim was not only shown the position of the wreck, but the medes were also carefully pointed out to him. 'If the wreck lies in the same position as it did, I'll be able to put you very close,' he told us confidently. But fate was to make one final effort to keep the secrets of the Shaalds just a little while longer.

It was a murky day when our two boats left the Voe together, and we had scarcely travelled a quarter of a mile when thick cloud started to envelop the south end of Foula. As we came near to the reef it was obvious we were not going to get our south mede: indeed, it was getting harder by the minute to pick out precise points to the north of the isle. However, with great skill, Jim was able to pinpoint his northerly marks, which meant that somewhere along that line, if his mede was correct, would lie the wreck. The south mede would have clinched the exact spot but we were going to have to do without it.

Alec, with his much keener eyesight and skilled boat-handling, was to stay up top once more, while I carried on with my spot dips along that north line. Time and again I went down—10, 11, 12 fathoms—and was rewarded with the same spectacular scenery. Everything but a shipwreck. By the time I had kitted up, dropped in, swum down, searched, surfaced and been picked up, and taken back to the north line several times, an hour and a half had passed.

Jim's careful timing had meant that the searching had started in favourable tidal conditions, but once the flood reaches the Shaalds it comes fairly belting in. We could try only once more, and for the final time we jockeyed into position and sent the anchor spinning over the side into 5 fathoms. Surely 30 ft was much too shallow to cover the wreck of a huge liner?

Nevertheless the anchor was fast on the bottom. I can't recall who realised it first but I think we both suspected that this was

3 (*above*) The library with its massive bookcase and Edwardian 'period' furniture (*Harland & Wolff, Belfast*);
4 (*below*) a corner of the elaborately decorated smokeroom (*Harland & Wolff, Belfast*)

5 (*above*) The machining of the colossal crankshaft of the *Oceanic* at Harland and Wolff's yard (*Merseyside County Museums*);
6 (*below*) one of the propeller bosses comes ashore at Scalloway. Each boss weighed slightly under 12 tons, and had to be carried all the way from Foula to Scalloway slung under *Valorous*'s bow. If anything had broken on the journey across – either a strop or a shackle – then several thousand pounds worth of metal and perhaps the boat herself would have been lost.

it. We both tend to be unemotional, but the knot came to my stomach in a flash. Yet strangely the feeling of excitement was mingled with an emotion that was probably fear more than anything else.

Scared? It's hard to describe, but several of my diving friends have experienced this feeling in similar circumstances. It's not a fear of the conditions, or a fear of going underwater, but rather a fear of the unknown. So many hopes have been built up; so many dreams have been dreamed; so many plans have been made. Was I going to land on a ship's boiler the size of a house? Or engines far more impressive than I had ever dreamed of? Or a massive, awesome propeller?

I was ready in an instant, for there was little time left. Fins kicked on; weight belt slung round my waist; spit on the inside of my mask to prevent it misting, and firmly pulled over my nose and eyes. Alec had the cylinders on the pontoon, with the straps adjusted ready for me to pull the set on. A couple of quick breaths on the demand valve partly for reassurance and partly to check the pillar valves were turned on, and I was ready. The anchor line was pulled in tight and thrust into my hand. 'Go!' shouted Alec and I plunged backwards, urgently pulling in the line so that I would get below the surface and away from the worst of the tide. As I pulled at the rope with my arms I kicked furiously with my fins, breathing in gasps—in part because of the physical effort but probably more from excitement.

The water cascaded past me. My arms were aching from the strain of merely hanging on to the rope. The tide seemed to be tearing the mask from my face, the valve from my mouth, and practically the very air from my lungs. Hand over hand, inch by inch I hauled myself down that rope. I peered ahead into this river, just waiting for the shapes on the bottom to appear. Another group of boulders? A rocky shelf?

I saw the weed first, streaming out and tearing at its roots. Sure enough, there's a couple of boulders and a shoal of piltock float by. But this isn't natural. Nature doesn't make straight lines. There they were disappearing into the gloom. The remains of

steel beams, rusted and made razor sharp by the ceaseless movement of the sea. I'm at the foot of the anchor, hanging on to
what was once a huge steel plate on the ship. I turn my head to
the right. There's part of a ship's side, with portholes still fixed
to it. I now know it's not just the remains of a small coaster, or
steel trawler, that has come to grief on the reef. I can't see much
but know I'm on the *Oceanic*.

First Robbie and now us. Forty-nine years apart. He could do
nothing with it, but how would we fare? I hung for a moment
and tried to control my breathing, my actions, my emotions. I
am bursting to surface and shout the news but there are things
to be done. Climbing across the bottom from beam to beam,
rather like a rock-climber but weightless and at the mercy of the
tide, I look around but always keep the rope in sight. If I lose
my way I will have to surface downtide, and Alec will have to
ditch the anchor to come to pick me up. Then the wreck would
still not be pinpointed.

I work myself back to the foot of the anchor line, but there
is one more thing I must do before I surface. I see a coil of
copper wire, some electrical fitting spiralling into wreckage. I
must break a piece off, twisting it one way and then the other
to fracture it. Our first bit of salvaged metal. Round my neck
was the noose of a compass and depth gauge (always carried
when searching operations were being carried out). It's caught
in the copper and I'm hanging by it like a high flier in a circus.
I haven't the strength to pull myself forward, so strong is the
tide. I reach to my belt and carefully pull my knife from its
sheath. I cut the noose and suddenly I'm free again, and moments
later have worked the copper loose. With the rope slipping
through one hand I make for the surface. I'm completely elated,
but too involved in simple things like breathing and hanging on
to shout about it. The demand valve is still clenched between
my teeth, rather like a boxer's gumshield, and wordlessly I hand
up the piece of copper. That says it all. It's a token gift to Jim,
the first piece of scrap from a wreck that had been on his
doorstep all his life, and yet deemed undiveable by the experts.

He had contributed much to putting us there, and he would treasure the first piece. There was plenty more for us.

There was no time for heroic gestures, tears or noble speeches. The quickening tide saw to that. Another rope with a buoy fixed to the far end was given to me, and this had to be attached to a sturdy part of the wreck. We would then have a buoy floating on the reef for the next dive, and we could moor up to it easily without the complication of looking for the medes.

There is one golden rule to follow if you want to work on a shipwreck, and we hadn't obeyed it. You must recover one 'official' piece of metal. I tied our new mooring to a lifeboat davit, long collapsed and splayed out on the bottom like a fallen tree. I quickly found the gunmetal casing of a decklight. Recover one piece of metal from an abandoned wreck, declare it to the local Receiver of Wrecks at HM Customs and Excise, and you can claim to be Salvor in Possession of the Wreck. It's a legal term, but it was to be vital to us as we were very soon to find out.

I dragged it over to the anchor, which I freed with considerable difficulty as the tide was now very fierce. Hanging on to nearby wreckage with my legs, I threaded the anchor twice through the casing and tied it off. I yanked the rope violently, and received an answering pull. It meant: 'Are you ready?' and the pull in return meant 'Yes'. I gave two pulls, which were returned. This meant 'pull up' and the two in return meant the message was understood. Anchor, load and diver came off the bottom and, despite all this weight, the tide had us streaming away behind the inflatable. Soon however man and load were aboard. I was exhausted but we were both grinning from ear to ear. 'There's a bloody big ship down there!' was all I could gasp, but somehow it seemed to sum everything up.

The most valuable non-ferrous fittings on a steamship are in her engine and stern section, so the full implication of what we had hit had still not really registered with us. The wreckage was so smashed up and overgrown with thick, heavy weed, that it was hard immediately to work out just where the engines lay.

At the time we did not know which direction the ship had been facing when she ran aground.

So the following day, not knowing how the ship lay, we threw the anchor over the side of the inflatable close to our permanent mooring. The engines were our prime target, but we were not to find them yet for the nicest possible reason—there was so much other loose scrap elsewhere!

I pulled myself down the rope to the new location and looked around me. It was as if the great ship had been smashed by bombs. We had seen on television some years earlier the massive *Torrey Canyon* on the reefs off the Scillies, and how the RAF were called in to flatten the floundering tanker with tons of bombs. No bombs were needed for the *Oceanic*. Just one 12-hour north-westerly Shetland gale had done the dispersal job.

At this point I'll ask the reader to look at a photograph of the *Oceanic* (page 33) and just imagine it under the water. You will have the popular concept of what a sunken ship looks like, an image created and nurtured by Holywood films. Perhaps you will imagine the diver swimming up the side of the ship, down a passageway on the deck, round a massive funnel and on to the bridge. Perhaps later he will go inside the ship itself, nosing into cabins or those wonderful staterooms, while all around seeing the signs of a quickly abandoned ship.

Well, forget it! Perhaps there would be some truth in such a picture on a deep-water wreck—like the *Titanic*, which I would expect to be fairly intact, protected from the worst effects of crashing seas. To get a vivid picture of what the *Oceanic* actually looks like, remember that the ship didn't sink—she broke up.

As the diver pulls himself down the mooring rope, first of all he sees nothing but swirling water. If he is near the stern he will then see the propeller shafts—no sides, no decks, no holds, or anything like that. Now the propeller shaft is in the very heart of a ship, so when I say there is nothing above it then that will indicate just how broken up the ship was. This was ideal for us as the fittings were either broken off or accessible—easy to salvage.

Only the heaviest things remain—perhaps a winch, or a bollard (most of the massive boilers had disappeared), the propellers, the shafting, the engines, or a lifeboat davit. Bits of the sides of the ship remain, but in a totally incoherent form, and often difficult to recognise. Weed and other growth largely conceal scattered wreckage, while sand, shingle and the remains of the spacious coal bunkers conglomerate like a concrete round other parts.

So the diver isn't swimming inside anything. He is moving from spot to spot, noting where valuable fittings are. There is nothing above the engines, and occasionally he will ease himself cautiously and gingerly into gaps among the engines to get a valve or a pipe. We even swam round *inside* one of the cylinders (which gives you some idea of the size of the engine)!

It can be very difficult to tell people graphically just how powerful the sea can be on a shallow site—you just have to see a mighty steel beam twisted like a string of spaghetti, or the foaming, cascading water leaping perhaps 100 ft up as a wave breaks on the Shaalds during a heavy south-westerly blow. We are, in effect, diving in a badly stacked scrapyard, with the best lumps always in the most awkward positions!

But back to the initial recoveries. When once again I was on wreckage, it was nigh impossible to pick out a pattern or an indication of just how the wreck lay. The visibility was splendid—perhaps 40 to 50 ft—which would be nothing exceptional in the Mediterranean, but is most unusual for British waters that can often seem like dirty pea soup. We timed our slack tide more accurately as well, so the diver wasn't simply spending his time hanging on for dear life. For the first time I began to realise just how valuable and incredible our find was.

I surfaced and held on to the inflatable, where Alec anxiously asked me if there was any sign of the engines.

'No! No sign of them. We're still on wreckage but I haven't a clue where we are,' I replied.

'Shall I haul up the hook and try again?' he asked.

'No! Just hang on where you are. I may not know where we are, but there's scrap everywhere. We'll soon fill the boat.'

It was an incredible sight. A young child at Christmas time might dream of being let loose in a toy store to gather anything he wanted. The chances are that for the first moment or two he would be so excited that he would run round in circles, surrounded by so much that he wouldn't know where to start. For a moment I was like that young child in our own private Aladdin's cave. Every time I wrestled with one piece of scrap, I would see another more tempting bit out of the corner of my eye!

Many divers have a slang word for non-ferrous metals. Tut. And there was tut everywhere: pipes, valves, portholes and hatches were strewn about, just a few feet from our mooring. On a sheltered deeper water wreck you would expect much of it to be still attached to the wreck itself, but such had been the force and persistence of the sea in half a century of storms that much of it was just loose, begging to be lifted.

And thus the salvage of the *Oceanic* started, salvage work that was to break records in its own limited field started with the simplest possible technique. 'Pulley-haulies' we nicknamed it. The diver would attach a fitting or fittings weighing maybe up to a hundredweight (a bit less, by my request, if it happened to be me doing the hauling!) and then give the rope two hard tugs. The boatman would start to haul the scrap in, and the diver would follow the lift to the surface.

There the diver would grab the side of the inflatable with one hand, and with the other help haul the rope, since it was the boatman who had to do the real work, and the lift would be marginally heavier when it came out of the water. The critical point in the operation came when the scrap arrived at the surface. Often it was jagged and sharp, and the diver had to keep it clear of the inflatable rubber pontoon. It was awkward too for the boatman leaning out over the pontoon as he could not position his body directly above the lift. So nearly all the strain was taken on the forearms, and soon they had developed to make us look like a couple of Popeyes!

Swiftly the boatman unhitched the scrap, giving the diver the end of the rope, and he dived for the next lump. In the next few seconds the boatman had to find a spot in the already crowded 13 ft 6 in boat for the scrap. By this time the diver would have another haul ready and, after an exchange of signals, the operation would repeat itself.

Speed was essential, for at any moment the tide would start quickening and stop the diving. Indeed, I note from an early entry in the diary Alec's comment that on one dive he found the tide was ebbing to the north and by the time he returned to the bottom only a minute or so later it was flooding south.

We got more than 12 cwt within 20 minutes on that first recovery tide. Even with careful stacking of scrap we must have presented an odd sight as we came ashore. Copper pipes were sticking out at odd angles, and diving equipment was crammed between the scrap and the rubber pontoons to prevent damage. With our gear and the two of us perched awkwardly on top, the little boat was grossly overloaded, and we nudged the 2 miles to safety with difficulty.

But the feeling of elation and pride was memorable. Because of the bonanza metal prices of the time we had recovered between £400 and £500 worth of metal in our 20 minutes on the reef (a bit better than the clams!) and although it was not ours to sell it was a marvellous start. After a long, slow and careful journey we came to the pier at Foula, where we were greeted by Harry Gear who runs the post office. He had been born during the short spell that the *Oceanic* was on the rocks in 1914. He was amazed at what we had recovered. 'After all these years I never believed that any of the ship would be recovered,' he said. 'I was sure it was on the Shaalds for keeps.'

With such success on our first real recovery dive, we were raring to go on the day's second tide. The tide slackens, stops and increases in the opposite direction approximately every 6 hours 20 minutes, though somewhat confusingly the Shaalds doesn't turn at high and low water but rather at midtide. Although on occasion we were to manage three trips to the Shaalds in a single day—and on one bonanza day even four—we normally found that two trips in the day was all we could efficiently manage.

We had to lift the scrap on to the shore, carry our heavy cylinders to our base compressor for charging up with air, refuel our tanks, start breaking up the scrap, attempt to dry our suits, feed ourselves and, if we were lucky, have a quick breather, before racing to catch the next tide. It was a tough schedule, but we were new to it and the incentive of our first haul meant we were nosing our way out of the Voe to the Shaalds in good time.

Our first lesson was that it was not all going to be plain sailing. There was a breeze from the south that day which meant that with our first tide, the ebb, the wind and tide were travelling in the same direction—a lee tide. But on the second tide the wind and the flood tide were travelling in opposite directions (a weather tide). On that first tide the wind was of no real consequence and sea conditions were fine—six hours later you would not have believed it was the same day and the same place.

It looked really evil. With the conflicting forces on the shallow reef the chop and turbulence made work virtually impossible. Great walls of water built up on the reef, subsiding just a moment before they seemed ready to break and come crashing down upon us. At the end of one season we did risk quick dips in such conditions to recover our mooring buoys—they would never last through the winter gales—but the danger in such marginal conditions was to the boat and not the diver. We got our buoys, without incident, but it was like tip-toeing to the edge of a volcano which could erupt at any moment. It was a real and not totally necessary risk, and as such was basically unprofessional.

Much of salvage work at this level entails weighing up all the conditions and deciding exactly what risks you are prepared to take—in fact weighing up the odds. We decided early on that there were quite enough problems without stretching the conditions we would deem diveable, so we returned that day empty-handed. But there was a healthy forecast on the radio for the Fair Isle area, and with the lee tide in the morning we were confident that we could double our recoveries.

Lesson No 2 from the Shaalds. We awoke early to silence outside. Often the rattling and banging of the wind on our rickety house would give us the message that diving was out of the question, with the bonus of an extra hour or two in bed. When we looked out from the house, however, we couldn't even see the pier 60 yd away—thick fog. With no medes to work from it is almost impossible to locate a single buoy nearly 2 miles out to sea, but such was our keenness that, with Jim Gear's help, we tried.

Using a compass and a watch we marked off our course to the Shaalds, and when we had run our time we did box searches (run north for a couple of minutes, west for the same time, followed by south and east). Jim was also able to use his experience of the confused tidal patterns around the shallows on the half-mile reef to help pinpoint the site for us. It was all to no avail, and slightly frightening, for you to realise that you are in a very small boat in a very big sea, particularly when there is poor visibility. We made our way back to Foula which, fortunately, at 2 miles long was a somewhat easier target than a single buoy, but still very missable if we got our times and directions wrong.

We hit it all right and, with a fixed point marked, tried again—with the same lack of success. In fact we were later to decide that the risk to the diver in fog was too great—a boat had only to break a mooring and have engine trouble, and we very probably would have lost a diver with little or no chance of making his own way to Foula. Only once were we to break that rule—in exceptional circumstances—and again it was a calculated and necessary risk.

Although the weather was now against us, we had seen enough to decide that salvage work was possible, and the next move had to be an attempt to buy the wreck of the *Oceanic*. If we succeeded we could legally sell the metal we had recovered. Remember at this stage we knew nothing of the ownership and the history of the *Oceanic*, so we wrote to Mr N. Rowden at the Department of Trade Shipping Policy Division in London.

We have never met him but he is a most unusual type of civil servant. No matter what your query, his answer, decision, advice or price comes winging back to you in no time at all, typed out I suspect by himself. He is a good man to deal with, one of a very rare breed—a civil servant who will make a firm decision and give a straight positive answer—and the fact that the subject is the intricate one of war losses and marine salvage makes it all the more unusual that negotiations and paperwork are so simple.

It was September before we were to get a written reply from Mr Rowden, but this was because of the slowness of a letter and reply via the Foula mail-boat service which runs once a week at best and often much less frequently in autumn and winter.

We were determined to continue work and recovery whenever possible. The 28th was favourable, and in the morning we learned Shaalds Lesson No. 3, best summed up in the hackneyed phrase 'Time and tide wait for no man.' Very roughly, midtide at the Foula pier is slack water out on the Shaalds, and combining that with the local tide tables published each year by Harry, a Lerwick barber, we would plan our working timetable.

It was never as simple as all that, and I recall an old Shetland fisherman once telling me: 'The more you get to know about the tides on the Shaalds, the more you'll realise just how little you really know about them!' All sorts of factors—such as the direction and the speed of the wind—could vary the slack times, and that day we got our calculations wrong and arrived just as the tide was pulling away. There was nothing for it but to make our way back to Foula and wait six hours for the next one.

As on our previous dive we were after the engines. Again we slung the hook on a promising looking area, and again there were no engines. But once more there was a load of scrap just lying loose ready for lifting. It was a semi-submerged inflatable that picked its way very carefully back to the Voe an hour or so later, manned by two exhausted but exhilarated divers. While I prepared a meal of Foula lamb, kindly given to us by a neighbour, Alec carried on with the chores of charging sets and unloading scrap so we could catch the early morning tide.

Our efforts were rewarded by six days of tearing gales. We pulled our gemini from the water and lashed it down. We lifted our gear clear of the pier. We shivered in our cold, damp house, where a puddle of water from the blocked drains lay in the sitting room. We tried to get our fire going, with smoke belching throughout the room, from peats kindly given to us by Harry, the island's most prolific cutter. (Coal was never burned while we were on the island—the only exception being a few lumps we dug up from the *Oceanic* site, just for fun.)

Other salvage men could sit in front of the roaring fire in the local pub, pint pot in hand, comfortably waiting for the weather to improve. Salvage work for us suddenly wasn't so much fun, and we began to realise some of the reasons why the *Oceanic* had remained untouched for so long.

But the weather moderated, and on 4 September we once more made our way out to the Shaalds where Lesson No. 4 awaited us. 'Moorings that will do for most wrecks, will have to be made of sterner stuff on the Shaalds.' The gales had taken our buoy, but we had the medes for the wreck and for the first time by ourselves we could test how accurately we could plot them. My eyes aren't that sharp, but Alec's come into the hawk category and within a couple of minutes our anchor was spinning on to the wreck. This time we were on the anchor chain, anchors, and winches—obviously a long way from where the engines lay. But again there was scrap lying loose all around, and we had to postpone our engine search while we loaded our boat. 'A bird in the hand is worth two in the bush.'

In the afternoon we prised another load from the same place. We were, too, becoming more cautious and limiting our loads to 6 or 7 hundredweight, which was actually plenty at one time. The following day's entry in the diary is concise. 'On engine room and boiler room. Lift 7½ cwt on first trip and 6 cwt on the next. Great day. Condenser with gun casing. Enormous bearings. Completely exhausted.' (The reference to gun casing is nothing to do with armament, though the *Oceanic* was armed, but to thick gunmetal casing on the condenser; in every other condenser either of us had come across the casing was cast iron. In fact we were to find on lifting the metal it was yellow brass and not gunmetal.)

This was the day that we were to realise that we were to be in Foula for a long time. We were getting the drift of how the wreck lay, and when Alec slung the hook over I soon found myself on top of three of the biggest boilers I am ever likely to see. Subsequent research showed us that they weigh in the region of 100 tons each (the *Oceanic* had 15 boilers) and a diver could easily swim right through the boiler by the stoke holds—and this diver, for the pure hell of it, did! The engines should have been directly aft of the boilers, but moving a little way off, keeping within sight of the boilers so I could return to the position, I was still unable to locate them.

It was altogether appropriate that Alec should find them. He has this great knowledge and interest in marine engines, and he would eventually have to take them apart. He went down, worked out how the boilers must have moved (yes, 100 tons of boiler will rumble about quite easily in a Shetland gale), and quickly made his way back to the engines. At first glance he could not work out whether it was one engine or both, as everything was thickly covered with growth and weed.

Slowly he made his way round the massive engines, noting with amazement and delight the piles of pumps, pipes, fittings, small bearings and small valves lying loose all around. The main engines themselves were intact but lying listed to starboard. His particular skill, which was considerably increased by our experiences on the *Oceanic*, is in removing the valuable big end and main bearings from engines, and he was thrilled to see the size and quality of metal of the *Oceanic* bearings. As a little bonus—as if we needed one—he came across three spare bearings lying neatly to the side where the engineer had left them. All they needed was a strop passed through them and a winch to lift them—they weighed about 7 cwt for each half shell. One minute's work that would be worth £1,000 in the scrap merchant's yard!

Alec has vivid memories of the first condenser he found—we were to locate and recover all four. 'I saw it was massive, almost like a boiler on a smaller ship, but I knew at once what it was. Everything seemed so big. There was this copper pipe half jammed underneath it, and I stopped to tug it free. As it came I noticed it scraped the casing which I was sure would be cast iron, and I thought that the copper had left its own mark on the iron.' (The marks on ferrous metals—iron and steel—and non-ferrous—coppers, brasses and gunmetals—underwater are different in colour and appearance, and can usually be identified instantaneously by an experienced salvage diver.)

'And then the penny dropped. I couldn't believe that the whole thick casing might be non-ferrous. My hands were shaking with excitement as I pulled out my knife and scraped various parts of it. Yes, it's brass,' he recalled. Our wreck was going to be far more valuable than we had ever dared dream.

Alec will explain later in this book basically how a marine steam engine works, and what bits of the engine we aimed to recover, but it is relevant at this stage to outline what a condenser is and the job it does. Imagine a cylindrical box of drinking straws lying on its side. The 'straws' in a condenser are brass tubes held in position by brass endplates, and each tube is also held in two brass centre plates. A casing or cover holds the whole unit in position. The cylinders on the engine are driven by high-pressure steam, and when this steam completes its cycle and loses its pressure it is pumped through the condenser. At the same time seawater is pumped through the tubes (about 3000 in each of the *Oceanic*'s condensers) and this cools the steam back to water. It is pumped back to the boilers, heated up, and the process continues. The unit has to be made of brass, as steel would quickly be corroded by electrolytic action with the constant movement of the seawater.

In fact the propeller brass and the condensers were to contribute well over half our total recoveries, so the brass casing was a major bonus. 'I just couldn't get over all the loose scrap lying around, just waiting for the first person to come on the wreck,' says Alec. 'There was to be a lot of hard work, study—and some luck—involved in dismantling the engines, but the loose fittings were just there for the taking.' A more detailed look round soon unearthed two more giant condensers, and a fourth had rolled some way off the engine beds, but remained almost intact and was discovered and recovered later.

One of our early fears was that word of our success would leak out before we could tie up arrangements over ownership, and at this stage there was a scare when a contact phoned Foula. There was a whisper that an Orkney fishing boat, the *Norseman's Bride*, was on its way up with divers. Fortunately it was just rumour, and indeed later we were to meet its skipper David Reid and his brother Albert, who at that stage skippered another top Orkney earner, the *Bountiful*. Both built up very successful businesses by enterprise and effort at sea: by working in worse weather than anyone else and pushing well-rewarded crews to their limits.

I suppose the diving rumour stemmed from their reputation of always taking a chance and an opportunity, and while we acquired something of a reputation of sticking our necks out a bit with the *Oceanic*, our enterprise was minimal when we saw the achievements and opportunism of the Reid brothers. We were to run into the *Norseman's Bride* again under sad circumstances, for she ran on to the north end of Fair Isle in a winter storm in 1975. Fortunately they were under the lee of the island, and there was no loss of life. The insurance company paid up, David Reid went on successfully to other ventures, and we salvaged the propeller later that summer. It's an ill wind. . . .

We also indulged in a bit of what in sporting circles would be described as gamesmanship to protect our interests. Nobody alive had seen the wreck apart from ourselves, and while the engines and one of the lifeboat davits did come quite close to the surface, we felt it would do our cause no harm if we could

(*opposite*) Side elevation of wreck showing shallowness of water

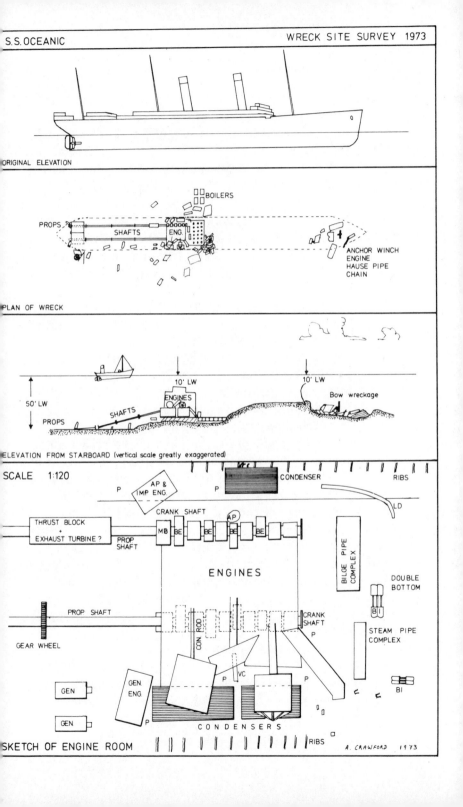

S.S. OCEANIC

WRECK SITE SURVEY 1973

ORIGINAL ELEVATION

BOILERS

PROPS

SHAFTS

ENG.

ANCHOR WINCH
ENGINE
HAUSE PIPE
CHAIN

PLAN OF WRECK

10' LW

10' LW

50' LW

ENGINES

Bow wreckage

SHAFTS

PROPS

ELEVATION FROM STARBOARD (vertical scale greatly exaggerated)

SCALE   1:120

CONDENSER

RIBS

P

AP &
IMP. ENG.

P

CRANK SHAFT

LD

THRUST BLOCK
+
EXHAUST TURBINE ?

PROP
SHAFT

MB

BE

BE

AP

BE

BE

BILGE PIPE
COMPLEX

DOUBLE
BOTTOM

ENGINES

BI

PROP SHAFT

CON. ROD

CRANK
SHAFT

P

STEAM PIPE
COMPLEX

GEAR WHEEL

GEN.
ENG.

P

VC

P

BI

GEN

P

P

GEN

C O N D E N S E R S

RIBS

SKETCH OF ENGINE ROOM

A. CRAWFORD   1973

indicate that they were just a little bit higher than they actually were. That way, if a rival heard of our successful activities and tried to hire a Shetland boat for a spot of plunder, his chances of getting a skipper to take him to the Shaalds would be rather less if the skipper felt he might crash on to an engine or davit.

We casually mentioned that some wreckage was very shallow indeed, and the grapevine started working. In no time at all, it seemed, tales were coming back of Shetland boats in the past that had been lobstering on the Shaalds, and had struck underwater obstructions. It must have been the engines of the *Oceanic*. . . . So a tiny exaggeration—not unlike Robbie's but with a different motive—and the power of word of mouth gave us some added protection. At no time in our five and a half years' work were we ever threatened by intruders—regrettably a state of affairs we could never have enjoyed in any other part of the country. More recently two amateur groups made contact with us to ask if they could come and see the wreck and we happily agreed—however in the final analysis the isolation of the island and the lack of regular transport meant they were unable to make the trip. So we had the wreck entirely to ourselves.

We managed a couple of tides on the 10th, and had a particularly good haul while Ken Gear was out fishing. Ken is one of the most widely known folk in all Shetland, mainly through the odd memorable incident during occasional wild sprees in Lerwick! Partial though he is to a dram or two and the high life, he also has a wide knowledge of tidal patterns, reefs and lobster holes around Foula's craggy shores. If there are piltocks to be caught around the Shaalds, then Ken will catch them, and we were fortunate to find him there at the same time as ourselves. He came over for a chat just as we were completing the loading of the gemini, and happily offered to take a load of scrap among the scores of wriggling fish in the bottom of his open Shetland boat. It seemed to take us only moments to fill our boat the second time, and so we had three loads for two tides.

Next day and next tide gave us another fright. We were coming in with our usual pile when the outboard engine all but

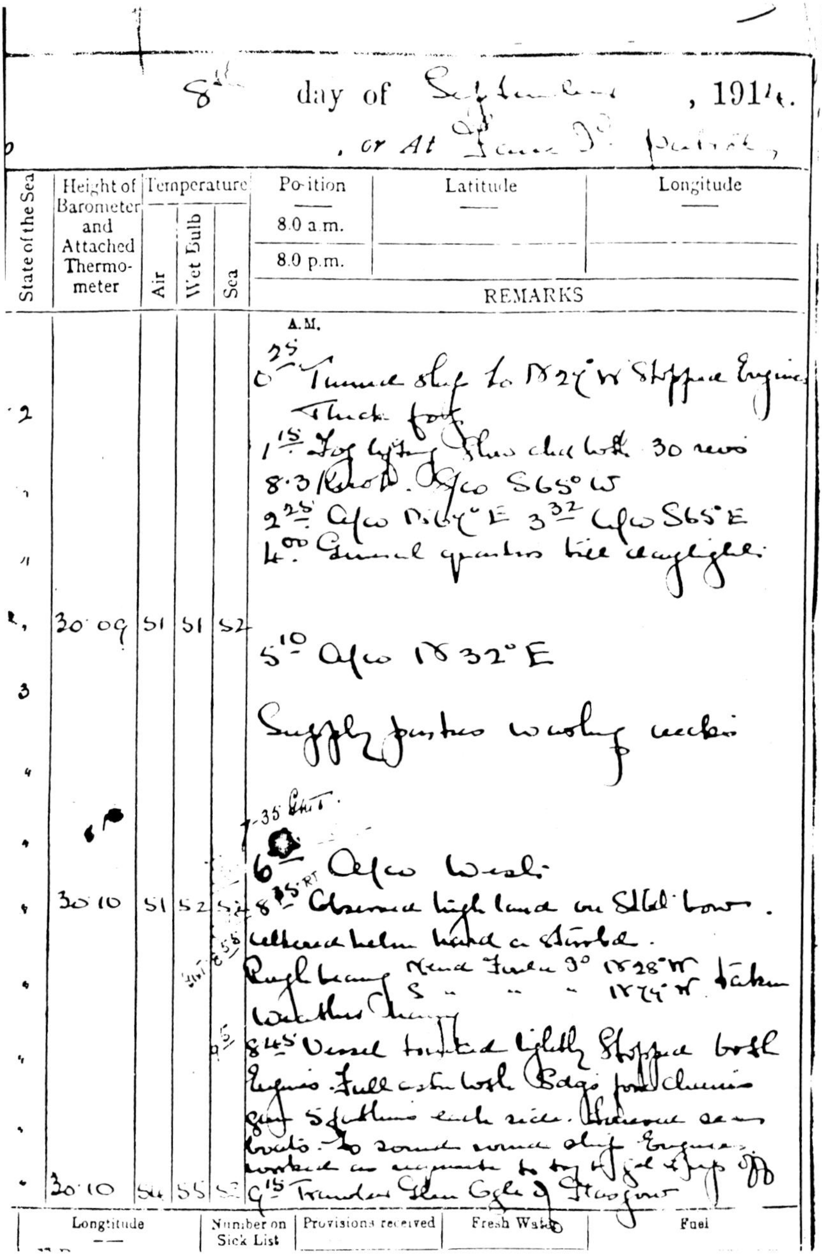

8th day of September, 1914.

, or At [illegible]

State of the Sea	Height of Barometer and Attached Thermometer	Temperature: Air	Wet Bulb	Sea	Position	Latitude	Longitude
					8.0 a.m.		
					8.0 p.m.		

REMARKS

A.M.

0 25 Turned ship to N 27° W Stopped Engines
Thick fog
1 15 Fog lifting. Proceeded both 30 revs
8.3 Knots. A/co S 65° W
2 28 A/co N 64° E 3 32 A/co S 65° E
4 00 General quarters till daylight

30.09	51	51	52	5 10 A/co N 32° E
30.10	51	52	52	8 35 Observed high land on Stbd bow.
30.10	54	55	52	9 15 [illegible]

Supply parties washing decks

7.35 [illegible]

6 A/co West

8 35 Observed high land on Stbd bow. Altered helm hard a Starboard. [illegible]

8 45 Vessel touched lightly Stopped both Engines. Full astern both. [illegible]

9 15 [illegible]

Longtitude	Number on Sick List	Provisions received	Fresh Water	Fuel

7 The *Oceanic*'s log for 8 September 1914. The smudges and unorthodox amendments can be seen on the lower half of the page (*Public Records Office*)

8 With no electricity – and no washing machine – we had to improvise, and Moya Crawford took the weekly wash down to the Ham Burn. Very nearly sharing her 'wash-tub' are the vertebrae of a 60-foot whale stranded in the Voe the previous winter.

packed up. The bush on the propeller had become damaged, and if Alec's temporary repairs hadn't enabled us to limp back to our base then we would have been faced with the prospect of heaving our hard-won loot over the side and attempting what would have been a very difficult paddle home in such circumstances.

A great comfort to us then was the knowledge that 'eyes were upon us'. Harry's job as Britain's most remote postmaster to some thirty souls with at most one mail collection and delivery per week could scarcely be described as arduous, but it is tying. Right from the start he showed a very real concern for our safety, and as the post office hut looked over the Shaalds he used to follow our progress closely with a powerful pair of binoculars. We were always very touched and grateful for that concern, and though mercifully his fears were never realised, it was a very reassuring thought that if something did go wrong the problems would be noted from the shore. As the years went by Harry felt more confident that we wouldn't do ourselves a mischief, but still kept the occasional eye on us. If we had had our own personal watching coastguard we could not have had a better surveillance than Harry gave us, and we are very much in his debt for it.

We managed to sort out that particular propeller problem, but breakdowns could easily be serious, mainly because spares were not easily available. We almost got round this problem in later years by carrying plenty of spares, but in emergency Sod's Law (definition—a piece of bread and syrup, dropped accidentally, will land sticky side down) usually applied and we had everything but the right bit. Even when we had the resources to maintain our gear to higher standards, equipment still caused Alec many a headache, and his experience gained from the harder times of botching and making do where we lacked the ideal tools and spares for a job was to pay many a dividend. It is a tribute to his work that never in five and a half years were we to miss more than one tide because of engine or compressor breakdown—a record that would be envied by many a two-week diving expedition.

In this case a 'botch-up' repair was done and a spare sent for and intermittently, where weather permitted, work continued. Soon, however, the emphasis for us was to change from mechanical problems to wreck politics when we learned from Mr Rowden that the *Oceanic* wreck had been sold by the Admiralty in 1924 to the Scapa Flow group—diver Robbie Robertson and his partners.

Local enquiries by friends of ours on the Shetland mainland indicated strongly that ownership of the wreck still lay with a Lerwick company. The matter was further confused by the fact, previously unknown to us, that while the *Oceanic* had remained totally forgotten since the abortive 1924 salvage attempts, that very summer an Aberdeen salvage man, Arthur Nundy, had made what was described as an 'exclusive' contract with the owners of the wreck to work, recover and sell material from the *Oceanic* for a period of up to five years.

We had heard, of course, that earlier in the summer two men had been up to Foula to do a survey of the *Oceanic*. They had hired a Scalloway fishing boat to take them to Foula and the Shaalds, but the fates had been as much against them as they were to be for us. For various reasons they were unable to get into the water, and I suspect that the skipper was unwilling to take his boat too close to the unknown shallowness around which the wreck lay.

Finally they arranged for Jock Ratter of Biggins to take them out there. Jock is a Foula man, born and bred, with a great love of the sea and would surely be able to drop the divers right on the site. But the day they arranged to go out with him the fog was down as thick as a hedge. On such a quirk of fate a whole story can hinge, and if that day had been clearer, the reader might now be reading *The Other Titanic* written by a different author. As it turned out, Jock and his passengers never went out to the wreck site.

Shortly afterwards we learned that the company which had purchased the wreck had been taken over by one of Shetland's major concerns, Hay & Co (Lerwick) Ltd. Armed with this knowledge we telephoned the Receiver of Wreck in Lerwick, declared the recoveries we had made to him, and asked him to mail us the appropriate forms—Foula somewhat unusually doesn't even have a local Receiver of Wreck. Then we telephoned the boss at Hay's and received, as our diary records, 'not a healthy reception'.

Andy Beattie is managing director of what was not long ago a small but diverse Shetland business. Since the coming of oil-related activities to the islands it has become a much larger concern. Having completed a salvage agreement with Nundy on an 'asset' that had long since been written off, he was not unnaturally displeased to hear rumours—as always in such cases exaggerated—that other divers were hauling rich recoveries from his wreck with not so much as a word to him. After our tense call, an appointment was made for a meeting in his office two days later.

On Monday it was blowing half a gale, and the mail-boat crew decided it was no weather to cross from Foula to the mainland. Alec and I felt our meeting was vital and it would not be in our interests to postpone it, so we risked a crossing in the inflatable. We dressed ourselves in our diving suits, put our everyday clothes into polythene sacks, and lashed ourselves for safety to the sides of the boat. We had a secure enough 18 mile journey, but were nonetheless glad to see the other side. We made our way to Lerwick.

Neither Alec nor I had much experience of business dealings previously, and we learned a lot from this particular episode. Both sides were poles apart—we were negotiating with the man who owned the wreck we were diving on and who was telling us firmly to get off it. We however were insisting that we would continue work. During the half-hour meeting, points were put resolutely but politely by both sides. Words were not minced but, in a situation which could easily have crumbled into a shouting match, a courtesy and dignity were maintained.

Andy Beattie is now boss of more than a hundred employees, but we later watched him extend no less time and concern to a crofter looking for a peat-cutting tool, than he did to a London insurance broker clinching a deal over a £1 million boat.

Because of this, when the way was clear in this complex and unusual case, there were no problems in clinching a deal that proved highly satisfactory to both sides. We were later to become good personal friends of Andy and his charming wife Edith, and they extended many kindnesses to us at their home in Lerwick. We were very pleased that they were able to fly into Foula in 1976, accompanied by senior directors of their parent company in Aberdeen, to see something of our operations out there. Their son Alan, a medical student in Aberdeen, also visited us and quickly picked up the basics of diving—we took him on a dip around the Voe where he saw many of the larger lumps which had been transferred from the *Oceanic* wreck site, ready for the final lifting.

At the initial meeting Andy pointed out to us that another salvage company was going to work on the wreck the following year and that we should leave it alone. We insisted that we were going to continue work, but added that if the matter came to court and we lost, we would then leave gracefully.

The meeting had its lighter moments. Andy compared owning a wreck to owning a car, and said that he could leave his car outside for as long as he wanted and it would still be his. We solemnly promised that we wouldn't pinch his car!

Alec and I returned to Foula without having achieved anything positive, but at least there was now a mutual respect and some further understanding between the two sides. By now it was getting later in the year and diving time was becoming even more infrequent, but we were soon to double our total haul in just two tides. Kenny McLennan was working, often single-handed, a 32 ft fishing boat called the *Lustre*, armed with a substantial winch. With such a small boat, so far out to sea and often 'hindered' by the close attentions of the Fishery Protection cruiser which protected the waters close to the isle, he was finding it hard to make ends meet. He is a cheerful character (he once steamed up to a cruiser and solemnly asked them for a fry of fish!) and is always willing to have a bash at something new. Couldn't he come out to the Shaalds a couple of tides with us, and lift some of the larger loose pieces that we couldn't manage by hand? We jumped at the chance.

We were aided by one of the slackest slack tides we ever experienced on the reef, and in no time we had recovered three spare gunmetal bearings, lined with whitemetal, weighing in total more than a ton. We also lifted some large pipes, a pump and some other bulky fittings.

Usually, when a diver gets a fisherman to do a lift for him, he has to coax and urge the skipper to give that extra little bit of pull on the winch. With Kenny it was the other way round. 'Oh! she'll take a wee bitty more' he cried as the boat heeled over crazily. Our final heavy lift was wedged solid on the sea floor, and Kenny refused to be beaten. The decks of the tiny boat were littered with great lumps of brass, making for even poorer stability. Ken Gear from the island was at the winch, Alec was in the water, and I was holding my breath with apprehension. 'Just a touch more and she'll come,' Kenny shouted, and then it happened.

I've never been on a fishing or salvage boat that has turned on its side, and I hope I'll never find out by experience just how far a boat will go over before it overturns. But I'm convinced it is no more than half an inch further than we were at that moment!

The winch and engine cut with the strain, and the tide, which was starting to flow, caught the boat broadside. There was a dreadful moment of utter silence. I was sure she was going. Water covered the whole of the starboard side of the deck and started to lap into the wheelhouse. In that split second between disaster and salvation, Ken managed to release the brake on the winch and the boat swung upright. No one would have drowned as the gemini was tied alongside, but the *Lustre* was within a whisker of landing on the *Oceanic*, which would have given Alec, watching on the bottom, quite a fright! We left our final lift for another year, but those valuable spare bearings were safely aboard.

We had now recovered and declared to the Receiver a total of 7½ tons of metal at an estimated value of £4,400, and such recoveries were inevitably putting pressure on the other would-be salvage man. We hoped he would take some action so that a situation which was turning to impasse would move towards a decision. Win or lose, we would then know how we stood.

Soon after this, first contact was made with Mr Nundy's agents. At this point I should state that at no time, either before or since the court case, did Alec or I have any contact whatsoever with Arthur Nundy directly and we have never met. It should also be said that while our court submissions differed on points of detail, he always appeared to be telling the truth as he saw it. For example, a lesser man could have claimed falsely that his divers had indeed located the wreck when they were out there and we might have been hard pressed to disprove it; such an assertion would have strengthened his position immeasurably. Salvage squabbles between rival parties can be messy affairs, but this one never was. Nundy must have been desperately disappointed with the outcome of the *Oceanic* business. Many a diving concern would have been much less frank in similar circumstances, and it is very much to his credit that he behaved as he did.

Our dealings with his representative from Glasgow were much less cordial, and quite different from our negotiations with Hay & Co. We were told in no uncertain terms to get off the wreck and, in the words of our diary, 'got the usual rubbish about putting the police on us'.

That heartened us considerably, for while we knew there was no guarantee we would win any court case we realised that it was certainly a civil rather than a criminal matter, and such a threat would only be likely to come from a position of weakness. If I were in his position and really thought I could get a rival carted off by the Boys in Blue then I wouldn't threaten—the first they would know of it was the knock on the door and the clink of the cuffs!

Two days later the man from Glasgow rang us 'without

prejudice' which means that the conversation and his offer could not be used in a future court case, which was fair enough. He offered us one-third net of our recoveries, with Nundy taking the scrap and selling it. In addition, we would agree only to work for that season, which was virtually at an end. It was strongly implied that if we rejected the offer court action would follow.

We thought things over and phoned back to Glasgow. We made things that little bit harder for him by stating that 'we would neither accept nor refuse any offer without seeing the contract between Nundy and Hay & Co.'

We dived for one tide on each of the following two days, which realised another 13 or 14 cwt of metal and cleared up one mystery. From the very start one of the most common questions put to us, very understandably, was 'what about the propellers?' We replied we didn't know and this time we weren't being devious. We were on the engines, and could clearly see the two shafts running off to the stern, but never made the swim. Why, many folk asked us?

Every single breathing moment we had on the Shaalds—and at that late stage of the season they were very limited—was devoted to hauling scrap. Every minute we spent looking about was costing us scrap recoveries. At any moment the full weight of the law could crash down on us and, though we were confident of winning any such struggle, defeat was a possibility. I was dying to look at the props, but we just could not spare the time. We had to get all the loose stuff as soon as possible before a court ban—which we thought was a real possibility—and in any case there was not much that two divers with an inflatable and a short length of lifting rope could do with two 29 ton monsters, still firmly attached to 30,000 tons of ship!

However, on our second last dive of the year, with most of the really handy loose stuff lifted, Alec made his way off down the starboard shaft. We were sure the blades would be brass, but the boss or centrepiece of many big propellers was steel—this was certainly the case in the *Titanic*, and the *Oceanic* in many aspects of her design was the same as her later sister. The boss would amount to about 40 per cent of the total propeller weight, and we suspected that the *Oceanic*'s would surely be of steel. Alec surfaced after his dip, let go his demand-valve mouthpiece, which enabled his grin to bring up somewhere at the back of his ears, and calmly announced: 'Brass on brass.'

The propellers were almost completely buried by wreckage, shingle and concreted conglomerate. The top blade on the starboard prop had been knocked off and was lying nearby, and the prop itself was almost invisible. The port prop was in the same condition, buried up to the boss, but this time the top blade towered upwards—almost 10 ft high. We would have some fun getting that apart, though explosives would be vital and at this stage we couldn't get any. Shetland police insist that a diver, even one experienced with explosives, has to have an agreement with the owner of the wreck before they will issue a permit. And we were a long way from that agreement.

With the weather getting more and more unpredictable, we decided we must try to get our remaining gear, equipment and clothes from Fair Isle. Our 'short trip' had developed into something much more significant, and everything obviously had to come to Foula. The Holbourns kindly allowed us to stay on at the Haa—our couple of weeks turned into five and a half years! However, there was no recognised way of getting from Foula direct to Fair Isle, and of moving the remainder of our equipment to our new base.

Encouraged by the success of our necessary trip to the Shetland mainland, we felt we could make the much longer journey of 44 miles to Fair Isle. The inflatable was a small boat to make such a long open-sea journey in at that time of year, but we carried plenty of fuel and a spare outboard engine. We took careful bearings before we left that Sunday, and were less concerned with the stiffish breeze blowing than we were happy with the clear visibility, which meant we should see either the towering cliffs of Foula or the lower 600 ft cliffs of Fair Isle for the whole of our trip.

Again it was a risky but necessary trip. We were aware it was really too far to go by inflatable, but what were our alternatives? The journey went without incident, apart from when we roared past some foreign fishermen who, judging by the alacrity with which they hauled in their nets, were up to no good and suspected we were a Fishery Protection 'snatch' squad! Tuesday saw us with our vehicle and gear on the *Good Shepherd* on its regular mail run to Grutness, near Shetland's airport at Sumburgh, at the south end of the mainland. From there we made our way up by land to Walls on the west side, where we knew that the Foula mail boat would be going home at the end of the week after the pony sales in Lerwick. We would then have all our salvage equipment on Foula and the Haa had a porch which, after repairs, would be ideal as a store for all our diving gear.

We reloaded our cargo on to the mail boat at Walls, and John Reid, the postmaster in the village, checked through the Foula mail sacks for our own letters. We suspected courtroom overtures would soon be starting, and if there were legal matters to clear up we wanted to deal with them before we returned to the isolation of Foula. There appeared to be no such mail. We left early for Foula in the inflatable, carrying Jock Ratter, who all his life had used the more sedate Shetland boats. He thoroughly enjoyed his fast trip and likened the planing inflatable to a maa (gull) skimming across the water—praise indeed from a traditional Foula boatman.

The mail boat arrived back on the isle late at night and it was not until about noon the following day that Harry came down with the mail and our interdicts. They were, of course, sent by recorded delivery and as such had been bound and sealed in a special sack. In less than two weeks we would have to have the replies before the Sheriff of 'Caithness, Sutherland, Orkney and Zetland', at Lerwick. Until then the message was very clear. If we dived on the *Oceanic* we would be breaking the law and be in contempt of court.

We had to see our lawyers in Edinburgh as soon as possible, and draw up our defences to the action. We had about four hours to catch the ferry south from Lerwick, and we were faced by the 18 miles back to Walls and a longer journey by road. I was leaving Foula for the year, so had to gather together my belongings before we left. As Alec prepared the boat in worsening and ominous conditions, I telephoned the Isbisters in Walls, who were to help us in many ways over the years, and they said they would have a taxi standing by. Once more we made the wet crossing, and Peter Isbister's daughter Iris was waiting by the slip in her taxi with the engine already running. We made the *St Clair* with moments to spare, and less than 48 hours later were sitting in a sombre lawyer's office in the heart of Edinburgh ... seemingly a million miles away from the Shaalds.

3

Salvors in Court

Picture a very common scene in the small-time salvage world. Team No 1 finds a wreck and starts making minor recoveries from it. Team No 2 hears about the find and recoveries—inevitably greatly exaggerated by pub gossip—and moves on to the wreck as well. Both dream of making their fortunes and, after heated exchanges (and sometimes worse), they all troop off to Court. There the matter is debated by lawyers and barristers in front of judges or sheriffs, all of whom dissect the nicer points of the law, but haven't the foggiest idea of the realities of an underwater wreck. (In one case in which I was involved—a Dutch East Indiaman—the legal profession appeared to have the idea that all the divers had to do was to shin down the rigging and look for the strongbox key!) After a while, with fees mounting all the time, both diving groups get a bit broke and the case is abandoned. The wreck proves to be almost worthless anyway. Only the lawyers win.

Having outlined that slightly cynical view of salvage disputes, let me say that the *Oceanic* was very different for several reasons. Here a salvage man, Nundy, had negotiated a deal with the owners of the *Oceanic* and had a signed contract giving him 'the right to work on this wreck and to recover and sell material from her'. Likewise we were not talking about potential 'might be' recoveries, but about real assets, as by the time the legal machine started rolling there were considerable metal recoveries on dry land.

Salvage law comes under a civil rather than a criminal heading, which means that the initiative to take the matter to court must come from one of the parties concerned rather than from the police. The law relating to the recovery of material lost at sea is complicated and dated, to say the least, as the Merchant Shipping Act relevant to such matters was drawn up in 1894 when salvage practice and problems were very different from those of today. As in other legal matters, much of salvage law is based on case history, but salvage case history is thin on the ground and the precedent normally consulted is the *Tubantia* case, heard at the Admiralty Probate Division in 1924.

The *Tubantia* story would merit a book on its own, for it is certainly a picturesque tale, but it is only the subsequent court case over the salvage dispute that is directly relevant to the *Oceanic* affair. It is a story in which it is often hard to separate fact and rumour. In 1916 a neutral Dutch steamship was torpedoed in the North Sea and settled in over 100 ft of water. The Germans were found to be responsible at a subsequent enquiry, and paid out considerable compensation.

There are some people, however, who feel that the Germans were cleverly framed by the British, who actually did the dirty deed. The ship's manifesto showed she was carrying an undistinguished cargo, mainly cheese, but rumours after the war suggested the German royal family were moving personal wealth out of a country that faced defeat and internal revolution. It was further rumoured that, as the German and British royal families had close blood links, a deal had been drawn up to give the *Tubantia* a safe passage through the Channel. Somewhere the plan went wrong.

Whether or not there really was gold on the wreck doesn't matter, because rumour rather than fact is all that is required to set plans in motion. Certainly war hero Major Sippe and his group thought they were after something a bit more exotic than six-year-old cheese when they hired steamers, tugs, divers and salvage experts to go after the *Tubantia* in 1922. They located her that year and returned to the broken wreck in 1923. Likewise their rivals, Vincent Grech and Count Zanardi Landi, had dreams of a fortune in gold when they elbowed their way into the action in 1923. After a preliminary skirmish Sippe gained an injunction against his rivals, and they all adjourned to the lawyers.

The first company's counsel argued the case from every angle, touching on flotsam, jetsam and ligan; at what point a harpooned whale became the possession of the harpooner; when a fish was partly or wholly caught; and they even brought up *Keeble v Hickeringill*, a case concerning the frightening of a duck from a decoy in the lawful possession of the plaintiff!

The second salvage company questioned the right of the first to go on searching for the possible treasure, with a bare possibility of success, to the exclusion of the whole world. They further claimed that property lost at sea is an invitation to all and sundry to move in and try to save it, and the only case when such interference would be unjustified is when the property is in no danger and safely in the custody of the first salvor.

Some days after the end of the four-day hearing the president of the court, Sir Henry Duke, read out his judgement. He had decided in favour of the first salvors. He said the wreck was 'derelict' in the legal sense—not in the possession or control of any owner or person acting on behalf of the owner. He went on to say that it would be wrong to assume that the first salvors could not properly be in possession of the wreck simply because bad weather prevented them from being in constant contact with it. In these circumstances Landi was not entitled to attempt simultaneous salvage. (This was an encouraging remark for us, as there were going to be long periods when we couldn't reach the *Oceanic*.)

Sir Henry cited a Privy Council decision in another case:

> In the case of a derelict the salvors who first take possession have not only a maritime lien on the ship, but they have the entire and absolute control and possession of the vessel, and no-one can interfere with them except in the case of manifest incompetence.

In restraining the second salvors Sir Henry concluded,

> I know of no reason for supposing it to be other than wrongful to obstruct a salvor in the course of his enterprise so as to prevent his carrying it on, even if the obstruction is practised by one who is entitled himself to be a salvor.

From our study of the *Tubantia* case, which is recognised as case law, we felt optimistic about our position. Nundy could in no way be compared to Landi, who had tried to barge his way into the salvage operations, whereas Nundy had previously negotiated a perfectly proper agreement with the owners. But, we felt, Sir Henry's judgement had placed no real emphasis on the wishes of the owner, and far more on the rights of a salvor. Unless his ruling was overruled it would appear that the first salvor had the right to possession to the exclusion of all others. Nundy apparently hadn't salvaged anything from the Shaalds, and if you haven't salved something then you can't be a salvor.

We were required to make an answer to the case in two weeks' time, though it was only through the good fortune of the mail's coinciding with good weather that we were able to do so. Our fourteen days were reckoned to start twenty-four hours after the documents were posted to us and they could easily, at that time of year, have sat in the post office at Walls while we were storm-bound on Foula. Indeed, if the weather had been finer, the mail boat would have crossed to Shetland and come back on the Monday, two days before the court case, and we would have been in ignorance of the action against us. Even in the last decade Foula was totally cut off from the outside world for seventy-seven days.

Nundy made three applications to the Sheriff. The first was a full interdict to restrain Alec and me from removing, selling or interfering with any part of the *Oceanic*, or from selling, removing or interfering with any part of the *Oceanic* already salvaged. The second, as an alternative, was to grant a similar interdict to the first, but an interim version. The third asked that we be ordered to hand over to him any bits from the *Oceanic* we had already recovered. The last one, we felt, was really irrelevant as we had declared the material recovered (as under the Merchant Shipping Act we were obliged to) to the Shetland Receiver of Wreck, and though it was lying outside our back door it was technically in his custody!

The Sheriff granted the interim interdict and called for us to reply. In his application Nundy had outlined the details of the wrecking and ownership, and had stated that Hay & Co had given him 'exclusive rights to work on the wreck and to recover and sell material from her'. He also stated that without permission from them or him we had removed from the wreck a large quantity of material, and that we had repeatedly been asked to stop working on the wreck, but had refused to do so.

In spite of the interdict, our cautious optimism was considerably increased by the confidence of our lawyer who was to make unstinting efforts on our behalf. We quickly got down to work on our replies.

After outlining a few technicalities we stated:

The wreck of the *Oceanic* having lain on the seabed abandoned for many years falls to be classed legally as derelict, with the result that any person is entitled irrespective of contract but subject to due observance of rights which may have accrued to other salvors by virtue of prior possession, to dive and locate a wreck and to recover parts of the vessel or its cargo.

We also pointed out that when we dived on the wreck it was hardly in Nundy's possession, since we believed his only attempt to find it had failed.

After more technicalities about how we took possession of the wreck we added that the granting of exclusive salvage rights wasn't legally binding under current salvage law and practice. We disputed that we needed the permission of Nundy or the owners before carrying out salvage work, and insisted that as we were the first salvors on the wreck, we were surely entitled to the assistance of the court in keeping away anyone trying to interfere with us. We admitted refusing to stop work on the wreck, and explained that we felt we had a right to be there, and could claim to be exclusively in possession. Furthermore, we suggested that Nundy's action was an attempt, without just cause, to interfere with our rights as salvors.

We laid our replies before the court on the appointed day,

and the Sheriff gave Nundy till 20 November to make any adjustments to his original statement, in the light of our replies. At this point Nundy's solicitor made a successful application for an adjournment of two weeks, and a fortnight later another adjournment was allowed on the grounds that bad weather had delayed the mails coming from the Scottish mainland.

We were disappointed in the delay because we were anxious to resolve the question, though with frequent tearing Shetland winter gales salvage work was out of the question (such a delay in a calm summer spell would have driven us near demented). Nundy questioned our experience, and stated that we didn't have the equipment or expertise to salvage the wreck competently. He went on to suggest that we intended to remove the easily recoverable and valuable pieces of the wreck, thereby making it uneconomic to mount a properly organised salvage operation.

He also mentioned that employees of his who had been sent up to Foula had been approached by us seeking work with them on the wreck. This wasn't true, but I'm sure it wasn't a deliberate misrepresentation as we learned later that his divers had been approached on their return to the Shetland mainland by two Scalloway men. We refuted this allegation in our final replies and in our view it very much weakened the only argument left open to him—remember, the *Tubantia* case had indicated that a salvor's right of possession could only be challenged on the grounds of his incompetence. It would now be difficult for Nundy to prove this when he even appeared confused as to who we were. He was in a poor position to comment on our incompetence or otherwise.

Our second and last note of adjustments outlined our joint experience in such work, listed the equipment we had left on the seabed (and which, of course, we had had to leave when we were interdicted), and tidied up some of the detail in our previous statement. The way was open for a debate between the two parties, but at this point Nundy withdrew from the action. As a result there was no decision and no findings which could be used as future case law.

9 The author (*right*) and his partner, Alec Crawford, motor out in the inflatable. Most of the salvage work was done from this craft (*Colin Martin*)

10 The end of a successful dive. Alec Crawford looks with satisfaction at the recoveries (*Colin Martin*)

We too dropped the matter. The interdict was lifted and we were free to return to the wreck whenever we could. We hadn't won the case, but very much more to the point, we hadn't lost it. We decided not to make any application to the court against Nundy in respect of damages for loss of earnings when we were banned from the *Oceanic*; the dispute was ended with dignity, and he went on to other plans.

The way was now clear for us, and the excellent personal relationship we always enjoyed with Andy Beattie, then joint (now sole) managing director of Hay & Co, meant there were no problems in drawing up a new agreement. We were undisputed salvors in possession and had successfully defended our right to work the wreck, but our agreement now gave us the right to sell the material we had recovered, though not before the Receiver of Wreck had been paid a 5 per cent commission on the metal lying at Foula—a profitable deal for HM Government, we considered, as the commission was payment for keeping custody even though they never set eyes on the stuff because of its isolation!

One point that always slightly concerned us was how precisely to maintain our status as 'salvors in possession'. Obviously we couldn't be expected to hang on to our moorings during a gale—to take an extreme case—or even, as a two-man team, be on the reef every available hour, day and night. Equally, if we were away from the island during the unsuitable winter periods and a good day turned up then, could another diver move in and claim possession? We decided that if we could prove work was under way, and declared to the Receiver of Wreck at the end of each season our intention of retaining possession and of returning the following year, our claim should be strong enough to win a further court action if needs be. In fact, a decision in the Court of Session at Edinburgh in July 1978 seemed to prove that the position of the salvor in possession was stronger and longer lasting than we suspected.

The case was between a private diver, Richard Price, and Scientific Survey and Location Ltd over a Dutch East Indiaman,

De Liefde, which was wrecked on the Out Skerries, Shetland, in 1711. The basic facts weren't in dispute. SSL, who claimed to be owners under an agreement with the Dutch government, stopped work on the wreck in 1969. Price started to work on the wreck in 1973 and made various recoveries including 2,000 silver coins, gold ducats and so on. SSL warned Price off the wreck, but he refused to move.

Price argued that even if the company were the owners, he was still salvor in possession and could keep this exclusive possession as the vessel was derelict. SSL counsel successfully disagreed, maintaining the vessel was not derelict, and that having obtained the title to it in 1968, they had retained it from then on. Price was forcing on them a service of salvage for which there was no need.

Since SSL had done no work on their wreck since 1969, this seemed to suggest that our salvage rights over the *Oceanic* would stand for some time.

With our court action under way it was important that at least one of us get back to Foula to watch over the wreck, as although we couldn't dive on it a whisper had gone round in diving circles that we had found something exceptional, and a guard was vital. Cash, as ever, was a problem since we couldn't sell the brass we'd recovered, and we decided that the best plan was for me to get a winter job in Fife and earn enough for the pair of us, while Alec returned to Foula to do some vital repairs to the house. I would arrange equipment and gear for the coming season, keep in touch with our Edinburgh lawyer, and deal with the many mundane problems that had to be sorted out for the undertaking ahead.

Alec returned to the isle in November, after waiting for a week for a two-hour settled spell in which to make the crossing. The first day a Force 10 storm raged, and while on the following day the wind dropped, the storm had left a legacy of a long heavy swell that would be whipped into a maelstrom if the wind increased. The real danger in such conditions is in being thrown out of the boat, but Alec tied himself in and, after one narrow

90

squeak leaving the Shetland mainland, he successfully made the crossing.

The Haa was an ideal base for us, but there was a lot to be done to it to make life comfortable. There was a puddle of water by the window in the sitting room, emanating from underneath the house itself. The fireplace puffed smoke, not up the chimney, but through a wall cavity and back into the room. Earth had built up against the outside of the kitchen wall, and together with the blocked drains, the whole house was terribly damp. Many of the slates needed replacing, and the rhone pipes—which supplied our only drinking water to a small tank—had come away from the wall in places. The roof above the front porch, where later we were to keep our spare equipment, was also leaking in places, and water deluged through whenever it rained—an occurrence that seemed to happen more frequently in Foula than in any other place on earth!

The house had been used latterly only for short summer stays, and the last major repair work had been done in 1936 when the classic film *The Edge of the World* was shot on the isle, and the film-makers, like us, did maintenance work in lieu of rent. The film was based on a story set in the evacuation of St Kilda in 1930, an even more remote island than Foula, and the *Edge of the World* was really a nickname for Hirta, the largest island in that group. Since the filming, though, the name has also stuck to Foula.

The so-called 'glamour' life of a salvage diver seemed a long way off for Alec that winter as, armed with pick and shovel, he spent hours digging deep into the hard, rocky ground to expose drains that had been laid many years before and had long since blocked. As he cleared them, water poured out in a stream from under the house. In later years we were to bring up lengths of pipe from the south, lay them, and then close up the trenches.

Obviously something also had to be done with the fire, and Alec pulled that apart too, reconstructing it with old firebricks from a ship's boiler.

Over the years it was amazing just how many of the fittings

from the *Oceanic* were, by necessity, brought into service as parts of our temporary home. Our curtain rails were condenser tubes, and they were held in place by copper supports that had once been part of the ship's generator. We fitted a stove in the kitchen with a lum (stove pipe) that began life as a heavy copper steampipe on the great ship. We boiled our heavy, blackened iron kettle on the peat fire—our only method of getting hot water—and placed it by the fireside on a large brass nut that had once helped to hold a massive propeller blade in position. We installed a second water tank to catch the rains from the roof and brought it into operation when required with a brass valve that had done much the same job on the White Star liner. A heavy brass locking pin from a water pump was used to open the bungs of 45 gal drums of diesel fuel.

Other people also made use of the old fittings, and whenever we stripped down valves and pumps we put the small brass nuts and bolts, springs and washers into a bin. Foula is a long way from the nearest ironmonger or spare parts dealer and we encouraged the islanders to rake about in this bin for anything they needed. It always cheered us, when considering what the fittings would cost to make as opposed to their scrap value, that some of the small pieces would be put to work again—in tractors, boats, engines, or in the houses. Even the steel piston heads from pumps have been pressed into service on the island holding nets on to coles of hay.

Often we were asked over the years just what we did on Foula when we weren't diving, in a community that had none of the traditional entertainments. Apart from his labours on the house, I notice from the diary that Alec found time to teach himself to play the fiddle—including, of course, 'The Shaalds of Foula'—to write a good part of a book, work with the sheep, overhaul one of the three island generators, run with the island mail boat on one of its infrequent trips, and even: 'Cut Elizabeth's oats with a scythe and take it up to shed. Hard work. Snow on ground.' Harvest in the snow is just one of those things that can happen on Foula.

Foula, or Ultima Thule as it was known as far back as Roman times, rises imperially out of the water, and from the Shetland mainland the five peaks—the Noup, Hamnafield, the Sneug, the Kame and Soberlie—stand out starkly and characteristically. The cliffs on the west side vie with those of St Kilda as the highest sheer cliffs in Britain—1,200 ft of solid rock towering from the sea. Foula, or Fughley as it was also once known, literally means Bird Island, and with due cause. Tysties (black guillemots), terricks (arctic terns), allens (arctic skuas), and maalies (fulmars) wheel incessantly in the skies over the island, making it an ornithologist's paradise.

It is estimated that at the peak there are 500,000 breeding birds on Foula, including 70,000 pairs of puffins (the 'norie', or puffin, was the old nickname for a Foula man), and 10,000 pairs of 'bonxies', or great skuas, making the island the largest breeding colony of these rare birds in Britain.

It is the tremendous winds, though, rather than the birds, that I will always remember when I think of Foula—winds which would howl and funnel down from the hills. One recent gale brought recorded wind speeds of more than 150 mph (Gale 8 on the Beaufort Scale is 35 knots), and it blew down a stone-erected shed, overturned a tractor, and scattered every stack of hay on the isle. One sheaf of hay—so the story goes—turned up 30 miles away on the Shetland mainland!

The islanders accept this kind of wind as a normal event, but the sheer power of the elements never ceased to surprise us. Alec came back from a croft house one night literally on his hands and knees, and it had nothing to do with the hospitality—he was quite unable to stand against the wind.

One lighter episode concerning the wind occurred when a scientific establishment from the south of England decided they wanted some readings of weather conditions west of Shetland. With great difficulty and even greater expense they managed to reach Foula with both their equipment and a sectioned hut which they erected at the south end of the island. It was a somewhat chastened boffin who rang back to base a few days later to say that he hadn't actually got any figures yet, but he had arrived at the site that morning just in time to see his hut disappearing over the cliffs. . . . Perhaps they could read something into that, and in the meantime, could they send him up another shed?

The island's community varies in size between thirty and forty folk, most of them living in houses like the Haa with no running water or electricity, and some cooking on open peat fires. So in some ways it is a hard life, lacking many of the luxuries most of us would call necessities, but there is a freedom from worry and the pressures of a speedier existence. Coronaries and ulcers aren't commonplace, and many of the islanders who have experienced mainland life have made the decision to return. Casual outside visitors often make the mistake of equating a basic, simple life with slightly simple people. The cleric from a passing cruise ship who patronisingly pressed 5p into the hand of a young bare-foot island woman who was tending her sheep would have been surprised to realise she possessed a university degree every bit as good as his own—indeed, Foula has more university graduates per capita than anywhere else in Britain. Visitors to an unusual community like Foula can be brash and thoughtless in their approach, and I remember rushing to hide in the Haa while one sight-seeing invasion landed at the pier.

Moments later, I was aware of two old ladies studying me intently, their faces pressed hard against the window.

'Look,' said one in utter amazement, as if viewing a performing monkey, 'he's reading a newspaper.' No doubt if I returned the honour at her comfortable city home I would probably end up in jail. . . .

I think one of the reasons we got on so well with the Foula folk is that we came to the island to do a job of work and not to look at or study them. Because of this we quickly became part of island life and followed the traditions of helping and being helped as required, with no thought of payment on either side.

Latterly the school was four pupils strong, but Foula children go to a mainland school in Lerwick after the age of eleven. The schoolteacher doubles as missionary (as he is called) in the island's tiny church overlooking the airstrip. The other focal point on the isle—the shop—was on its last legs when we came to Foula and I remember Harry, dressed in oilskins, solemnly handing out tins as the water poured down on him from holes in the roof. For some years now the shop has been closed, and food arrives in boxes either on the mail boat or via the Loganair Islander aircraft when it makes a chartered trip, perhaps with a county official or a tourist, or taking the island's community councillor, John Holbourn, to and from his meetings on the mainland.

One of the most memorable days out with the Foula folk was always the 'cruie'. Most of Foula's sheep wander loose in the hills, unfenced and virtually self-sufficient. They are tended at lambing time mainly by four women, Francie Ratter, Sheila Gear, Ann Holbourn and Isobel Gear, but in the autumn they are clipped and the lambs taken away. Many of the sheep are almost wild, and are driven up and down the hills by a crowd of people and dogs while other folk block off favourite escape routes. Eventually—if all goes according to plan—the sheep are driven into an enclosure or cruie where they can be caught. That's the theory.

In practice it can be quite different. Usually an early start is planned, but often timekeeping isn't the islanders' strongest suit and it was always well into the afternoon before things got under way. Some of the dogs tended to be a bit daft, and the sheep speedier and craftier than most of the catchers. But it was an exhausting and exhilarating day, with the sheep tearing about on narrow paths high up on the cliffs and islanders demonstrating great agility, balance and seeming total indifference to danger in their efforts to keep the animals on the move.

I remember once darkness falling just as the sheep were penned up by the Sneck of the Smallie, away on a remote part of the west coastline and about a mile from the nearest road. The lambs which were to be taken away and sold had had a front and a rear leg tied together in such a way that they couldn't take a full step, but could only hobble along. This prevented the semi-wild beasts taking to the hills again but, as a result, the journey over rough country in total darkness with these hobbled sheep would have been impossible. Calmly we all settled down for a yarn to await the full moon.

Many of the hill sheep were as primitive and basic as I have seen anywhere, and occasionally you would catch one which had eluded all previous cruies, with the remains of perhaps four or five years' fleeces dangling from its coat.

The Foula sheep almost seem to have evolved their own distinct strain on the isolated island—just one of the unique features of this enchanting isle. Foula's remoteness made it the last place in Britain where the old Norse language was spoken, and to this day the Foula community still clings to the ancient Julian calendar. As far as the rest of us were concerned, Pope Gregory corrected the official mathematics in 1582, but somehow the message has taken a little longer to reach Foula, where Old Yule is still celebrated on January 6, the children having worked at their school desks as usual on December 25!

The last focal point on the island is the post office. It must be one of the last places in Britain to have a hand-signed pre-World War I £5 note in its till (cash seldom passed out of the island until recently), and a further unusual feature is that domestic mail deliveries aren't unknown at 2 am! Post office holidays don't really apply, and traditionally the postmaster retires when he's no longer able to vault the counter (the only way to get behind it). Stamps are kept in the safe—not, as Harry quickly points out, from any fear of dishonesty, but because it's the only place guaranteed to be dry!

Truly, Foula has a charm and informality all its own.

4

Peat Banks and Propeller Blades

Mid-March 1974 saw my return to Foula. The talking was over, the court action satisfactorily settled, and the agreement signed with Hay & Co by the end of the month. That was to be the easy part. Many sophisticated plans for salvage operations are laid, and many are the excuses subsequently put forward as to why those plans were not carried out. Hard luck stories are useless. It's the pile of recoveries at the end of the day that counts, and there were still many doubts voiced as to our chances of making major recoveries from the treacherous reef. But at least it had lost its 'undiveable' tag!

We had now gathered together all our equipment and invested in some better gear, and we brought it over to the island in the *Lustre*, loaned to us for the day. Also on board was our Hafflinger, a versatile little four-wheel-drive vehicle, which somewhat stole the thunder from a helicopter firm who two days later, for publicity purposes, brought in the first-ever Foula nurse's car because this was thought to be the only way to get a vehicle into the isle!

We invested in a new 25 hp Evinrude outboard engine as a safety precaution, and apart from a minor initial problem it was never to let us down on the Shaalds over a period of five years. Our one criticism is that the bodywork of the engine did not appear to be as sound as the previous model's, and another engine also hard-worked over the same period by a friend showed the same signs of cracking up. But five years' hard, reliable work is a good record for an engine nowadays, and mechanically it was first rate.

On the wreck again we concentrated on clearing up more of the loose copper and brass—each spring we used to have a little bonus as the winter storms always turned up 'new' pieces in areas we had previously cleared out. The Shetland police insisted that the court case be over, an agreement signed, and permission obtained from the owners for explosives to be used on their wreck, before they would authorise a permit. On such a job as we were hoping to do they were absolutely essential, so we were very glad when the formalities were over.

Our first swim down the port shaft—we had inspected the starboard one the previous autumn—produced a fantastic bonus. Imagine pulling yourself along the massive 26 in diameter steel shaft, with the tide tugging you back by the ankles, and the surge tossing you effortlessly from side to side, scraping you across slivers of steel honed to a razor sharpness by half a century of ceaseless movement. Every nerve in your body is alert, eager, perhaps slightly on edge. The bottom is a mass of thick stalks of kelp waving with the motion of the sea, spreadeagling across your facemask and half-blinding you. The adrenalin is flowing, and you are breathing hard from the excitement and effort.

Alec went on such a swim.

All around there were great lumps of steel covered in weed so it was difficult to make out just what was what. I suddenly found myself up against this large circular flange and I thought: 'A spare section of propeller shaft, partially buried.' And then I went over the top, and it didn't look quite the right shape. The truth dawned on me as I pulled out my knife to check the metal. A spare manganese bronze propeller blade.

(Incidentally one of the commonest fallacies we hear is that all non-ferrous props are made of phosphor bronze—they virtually all are manganese bronze. Try passing off your prop brass off to your metal merchant as a valuable phosphor bronze and see how far you get!)

Still finding it hard to believe it wasn't his birthday, Alec's eyes caught sight of another blade right beside it. And another!

And another! There's number five! And number six! With quick measurements and extensive calculations on the surface, we estimated them to be 4 tons each—24 tons of propeller brass, lying absolutely free, complete with bolt holes ready for a strop. There they were, lying in 30 ft of water, just ready for the taking. Subsequently we were to find that one of them had been knocked off the starboard prop at the time of wrecking, but inspection after recovery revealed them to be not 4 tons each, but 5 tons 17 cwt—each blade neatly marked by the founder, and varying slightly in marked weights as they were unable in those days to cast exactly the same weight each time. Slightly lighter blades had lead melted and pinned inside the cupped flanges to ensure the uniform balance of the propeller, vital for smooth running.

We had carried out a good survey of the wreck, and had a fair idea of what was to be done. The two props—an estimated 29 tons each, minus the single starboard blade—had to be broken off the shaft, lifted out of the hole, and the blades broken from the boss so we could do the lifts in parts. The whole operation on each prop would be best carried out with one explosive charge, for it is very much easier to break a prop with its resistance on the shaft as opposed to when it is loose, when a charge is liable to toss it up in the air a few feet without doing the job. The tailshaft liner on each shaft would be just forward of the prop, and sweated tightly on to the shaft, and would run inside the gunmetal sterntube. This would be a most complicated and laborious extraction job, but we had some experience of that particular work, and we thought the estimated 12 tons of brass and gunmetal would be worth it.

Next there would be picking around the rudder steering engines and the brass gear wheels (and spare) that moved the rudder quadrant. Forward perhaps 150 ft to the engine, and we would have the four main generators, the evaporators (used for converting seawater to fresh), the thrust blocks, the thrust block pins, the four main condensers, the airpumps, impeller pumps, bilge pumps. In the engine itself we would find the main bearings,

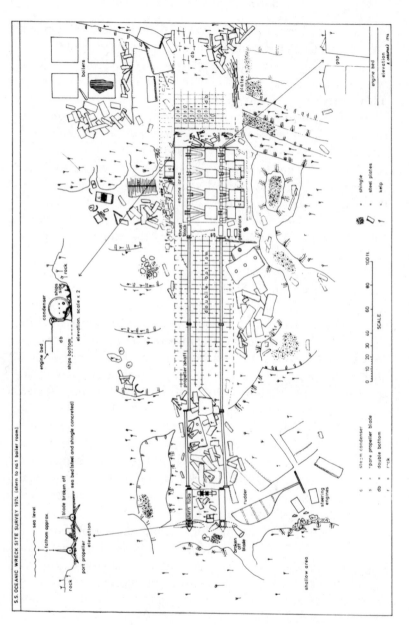

Detailed plan of the engine room and prop area, including spare propeller blades

the big end bearings, the small end bearings, the slide bearings, the eccentrics, and the multitude of smaller pumps, valves and pipes that surround any steam engine. More pumps and gear lay forward, right along the length of the ship to the bow where we had our eyes on the heavy brass teeth of the winches which lifted the huge 9 ton anchors. Listed like that the job all seems quite straightforward, but we were under no illusions that on such a reef and with so few days suitable for work, it was a task that was going to take several years.

Only a unit like ours could succeed in the job, for it was a tailor-made wreck for us. The bigger concern could never have got the returns necessary to pay a large labour bill and run expensive plant, bearing in mind there were so many days they couldn't work, while a couple of small-time operators like ourselves, prepared to move to a lonely island and forsake such luxuries as running water, electricity, time off and the bright lights would have a chance of success. Our efforts would have to be concisely and carefully planned. We would have to clear areas of all brass, before blowing down the massive engines which might bury it. Once the engines were down we could get at their valuable innards, though just one careless blast could at best set us back months and at worst cost us many thousands of pounds in lost recoveries.

It was while we were making our initial preparations for the year that there was an amusing episode involving the police. A quantity of diving equipment had been stolen from a firm specialising in contract work on the Shetland mainland. Such an incident was unheard of in the 1960s before the oil boom, but sadly now is much more commonplace. The local CID sat down to compile a list of possible suspects and, I suppose not unnaturally as we were an unknown pair working in Shetland, we figured prominently on the list.

Apparently the police planned a secret raid to Foula to see if we had the booty, but were faced with the problem of getting quietly to the island. You cannot roar up in a squad car to Foula. A plainclothes man went quietly down to the Scalloway café

101

innocently inquiring about the possibility of a lift out from local fishermen heading for the grounds to the west. Shetland may be remote, but the grapevine is second to none and within hours we were working on the Shaalds when a Shetland boat nosed up to us. 'They are planning a raid to see if you've got this nicked diving gear,' was the message.

Our consciences were crystal clear, but we were a bit concerned about our standing on the island if we were even indirectly responsible for an 'invasion'. Let me emphasise that Foula is a society totally without crime—any minor differences they are quite capable of sorting out among themselves—and indeed in all our time there was never a uniformed policeman on the island. It is a society away from officialdom and authority, and not overly concerned if the odd dog licence is a day or two out of date, but because of the liberal way of life the Foula folk are by and large very nervous of officials. 'Officials are fine if they come no closer to us than Lerwick' would just about sum up their feelings. So we spread the word around about this extra special hush-hush raid. It brought the memorable inquiry from one island housewife: 'Do you think if we rang them up they'd pop into the baker for some fresh bread for us?' Fortunately, before they could make their arrangements to come out and search us, they found their culprit much nearer home, and the 'raid' never occurred.

Early that year we sold our first load of scrap for £6,000 to realise some much needed cash. Our friends from Fair Isle came in the *Good Shepherd* to take a full 7 ton load to Wick, where it would be transported south by road to the markets in Glasgow. We were very touched when almost every man on the island came down to help us load, and within an hour we were making our way south in perfect weather.

We were quickly to learn that our valuable cargo, which could lie perfectly safely with our island friends from Fair Isle and Foula, would have to be watched all the time once we reached the mainland, right up to its sale at the market. We travelled down with the truck and stopped off on the way at a café which, we subsequently learned, had rather a reputation, rightly or wrongly, as a good place for things to fall off the back of lorries.

Alec and I were sitting there, tucking in to our bacon and eggs, a couple of scruffy, dirty young men after our sea trip and filthy job of moving scrap—looking anything but the owners of a very valuable load. 'What you got tonight then, Fred?' inquired the large tealady, whose eyes lit up like the winning line in a fruit machine when Fred our driver mumbled: 'Copper and brass.'

Alas, poor old Fred was a bit slow, and his face was a picture as he tried to indicate, by wink or grimace, 'Shut up, woman, I've got the owners here.' Of course there was no proof of evil intent, but we were glad we were there! The weight of our load had been checked at Wick, when Fred didn't know we were coming with him, and it had miraculously grown by ¼ ton by the time we got to Glasgow, so if we hadn't been there an equivalent amount could have disappeared on the journey without ever our knowing. We had put too much effort and risk into recovering the stuff in the first place to be anything but very unhappy at the thought of anyone nicking it at the last moment. On occasion, when a lorry had to stop for a night break, I have been quite content to foresake a warm bed in 'digs' to lie dozing under the axles, cradling a solid brass pumpshaft in my arms! Later we were to deal with Mr Steven's haulage firm in Wick, and always had the best of service from him and his friendly drivers—a far cry from the eventful early trips.

We returned to Shetland at the beginning of May with a tool that was to save us hundreds of hours of work. Previously in all our salvage career we had to 'break and clean' scrap—strip valves and pumps, take off cast iron, remove studs, cut off braziery flanges and so on—with axes, hacksaws, sledgehammers and wrenches.

While we were south we bought a Cutquick saw, which revolutionised scrap cleaning for us. We soon nicknamed it the 'zipper', as it fairly zipped through the non-ferrous metal and would easily cut steel as well. It has a petrol-driven engine and a rotating carborundum disc which rotates at great speed and cuts the metal. The disc eventually wears away and is replaced by another. Pumps and valves were inevitably twisted and warped after their years on the battered sea-bed. A pump that an engineer on the *Oceanic* would have taken apart in a few minutes would be almost impossible to dismantle when we salvaged it. The zipper just cut it into chunks.

We also offered £4,000 at this stage for a Shetland boat *La Morlaye* which was up for sale and would have been fine for salvage work, but unfortunately it was sold for a good bit more than we would have been prepared to pay. So we just had to continue with our basic work, doing some of the small-scale initial blasting, and concentrated further in getting the Haa suitable as a longterm base.

No coal comes into Foula, and all the island's main heating fuel is peat. Happily there is no shortage of this commodity, the island largely consisting of a peat bog on rock. Through the kindness of the islanders, particularly Harry, we had not gone short of peats in the early days but now we were planning to live semi-permanently on Foula we had to cut our own. Peat Marshall Rob Holbourn allocated two banks specially for us, at Sloag and Gossameadow, and each springtime for the next five years we prepared our banks, cast our peats with tushkars (peat-cutting tools) made for us by Jock Ratter, raised them when dry, raised them into piles, and brought them back to the Haa yard. Whatever the time of year we usually had at least one peat fire roaring, keeping the once near waterlogged house dry and enabling us to boil kettles for hot water when we required it. Getting in and out of wetsuits, on many of the islands we were on, could be a pretty cold and miserable operation, but not so on Foula with our peat fires.

Peat cutting Shetland style requires certain skills but we soon got the hang of it after a spell during which broken peats lay all over the ground. 'They all burn,' we were kindly told by the experts. In later years, however, we were to become quite neat

104

and efficient and on occasion joined 'the cutters'—a long-standing Foula tradition when all the able-bodied men were 'bid to the banks' of women who didn't have a cutter in the house.

We were also faced with the problems, on top of conventional salvage work, of ordering and preparing food and doing the bare minimum of housework. Diet is very important in arduous physical work, particularly with diving, where considerable heat loss is commonplace, and it was something we were determined would not hinder our work. The lack of fresh food was the biggest drawback, for we could get heartily sick of tinned food.

Towards the end of the summer we were often given fresh-killed Foula lamb, which tastes better than any other I have tried, and at the height of the summer the menu often included fresh fish with the smaller island boats out at the fishing and the Shetland trawlers sometimes calling in with a 'fry' of haddock so fresh it was practically wriggling. In the early parts of the year, when fresh food was really scarce, we lapsed into the habits of the old Foula and St Kilda folk, and such dishes as stewed shag (ugh!) and roast puffin (very good!) found their way on to the menu with many an unusual seabird omelette.

This chore was taken from us for most of the year when we got the first of our cooks, Deidre Yeoman, who had been working on Fair Isle at the bird hostel the year before and who wanted a chance to see life on Foula. She would have a lot of free time to move round the island studying the multitudes of birds, many of them rare, though such was her versatility that she was to be of great help on occasion on deck during salvage operations.

Alec had a bit of an adventure going across to Shetland to pick her up, encountering fog and visibility of just a few feet on the mainland side. Fortunately Shetland is a bigger target than Foula, and though he went slightly off course he knew he would hit land somewhere. He was more than a little startled, though, when he pulled up on a lonely beach, asked his position at a croft house he found some way off, and found he was no longer on the chart!

Alec had been hard at work designing gear that would help us lift heavier weights, up to 3 cwt, directly into the inflatable, and had knocked together an A-frame bracket contraption that fitted on to the stern of the craft. We removed the outboard engine while moored over the wreck, and with blocks and rope tackle we managed to lift such weights inboard. But it was still not enough, and we could not go ahead with any major blasting work until we had a boat large enough to lift the large lumps of brass we had already loosened and uncovered. As Alec noted in his diary: 'Scrap running dry and frightened of blasting until the larger pieces are removed. Slight surge and poor vis, port condenser area quite dangerous now.' That was putting it mildly, but still the temptation was there if you saw a fine bit of scrap buried deep, to go in after it in spite of the risk of collapse.

By the end of June we got our second load of scrap away, again with the help of the *Good Shepherd*, and we moved it south without incident. With this second cheque of the year safely in the bank, we were now in a stronger position to buy ourselves a boat capable of the big lifts facing us. We would obviously have to compromise, for at such short notice with only reasonable funds, the perfect boat was out of the question. We hared round every east-coast port from Wick to Kirkcaldy, inspecting boats, and we made two or three offers. It was all to no avail.

We had also been scanning the advertisements for the sale of boats in *Fishing News* and there, tucked away in a corner, was a small ad. for an old 50-footer lying by a quiet pier at Peterhead. We called there for a close look.

Trygg was a Norwegian-built boat, constructed before the outbreak of the last war and, traditionally, very heavily built in pine. She wasn't a beautiful boat to look at, and was obviously much nearer the end of her career than the beginning. She had a distinguished history, particularly through the war years. She undertook several secret and highly dangerous missions between German-occupied Norway and Shetland, carrying agents into Norway, and personnel out of the country when things got too hot for them. Many boats and people were lost on hazardous missions, and while we don't know precise details of her exact movements, *Trygg* distinguished herself.

It was an ironic twist of fate that she was to return to the scene of some of her great triumphs with us some 30 years on. From a distance she did not look at all promising. For a start she was not rigged with a mast or derrick, and she had the traditional heavy, large wooden rudder. She was festooned in rubber tyres all round her gunwales, protecting her from buffeting on harbour delivery runs. She had a very wide beam of about 18 ft, which would be a considerable asset in lifting, but would make her lively. There was no gear aboard except for a VHF radio and a compass.

She had, however, several advantages over the fishing boats we had been looking at. She had no trawls, nets and other fishing gear a buyer of an old boat often inherits with his new purchase, making the boat itself a cheaper buy. She had a spacious hold with a wide hatchway which would be essential for loading the large lumps of condenser housing, and a sturdy 1 ton Fifer winch. The bottom of the hold had tons of concrete poured in as ballast which would make a sound base for the jagged pieces of scrap to lie on. Lastly, her Norwegian name meant 'safe, or secure', and whatever other problems we might have with her she looked a safe boat.

A slight problem was that there was £1,500 difference between the asking price and our offer, but we knew the firm that owned it were very keen to get rid of a boat which had been on the market for some time and was surplus to their requirements. With a bit of give and take we were soon the owners of the vessel. She was to be an absolute snip for us, and was to do an immense amount of valuable work—and never, never let us down.

We collected a tiny, stub mast and derrick from the shore, and did some hurried welding and extension jobs which would allow simple and relatively light lifts for the rest of the season. Although she was an old boat and, not surprisingly, rough in places, essentials such as the Kelvin T4 120 hp engine had been well looked after by retired Peterhead skipper Jim Buchan, who was to give us invaluable help and advice on the boat's characteristics. Three days after we bought *Trygg* we were safely in Foula. Luckily we had clear weather—without radar, looking for such a tiny island in such a vast expanse of sea, would have been well-nigh impossible had we encountered a thick fog.

It was out of the question to lift single castings of 6 tons and more directly inboard—we would need a much bigger boat for that, more powerful winches and so on, and apart from anything else, the bigger boat couldn't stay at Foula or even get on to the shallow reef. So Alec designed a block and tackle system that would lift the propeller blades to within a few feet of the surface from the bow of the boat. From there we could take them in to the point of the pier, drop them, and with yet another block and tackle system, drag them under the pierhead crane, using the winch that hauls the island mail boat up the slip.

When each blade was underneath the crane, but still in the water, the winch-wire would be reconnected to the crane itself, and the blades lifted ashore and clear so as not to hamper the retrieval of the mail boat. Then, on a very high flood tide, our salvage boat could be taken in under the crane, with the bows resting on the rocks while one or possibly two blades would be lowered into the hold. Altogether, the removal of 11 blades would prove a considerable operation.

For safety, the main triple lifting block would have to be tested to a 24 ton load, and a new block like this would cost several hundred pounds. We had to cut a corner, and once we knew the *Trygg* was ours, we took off to the ship-breaking yards of the Forth—where, incidentally, so many of the scuttled German ships from Scapa were broken up, and the *Titanic*'s sister, *Olympic*, ended her days. After several hours digging in piles of rubbish we came up with the perfect block, together with a spare should we lose the first. We also found a hefty double block which would complete the rig at water level. Then we moved to other scrapyards to get suitable wires for the job—the Royal Navy, the Post Office, and the mines throw away some super stuff in Fife!

Initially our plans were to get the boat ready, properly rigged for lifting, and this work took precedence over other salvage operations. The winch mechanism had seized solid through lack of use, and a lot of hard effort was needed to free it. We were also to learn quickly, the hard way, that Foula pier is an almost impossible place to keep a 50 ft boat for any length of time.

Trygg drew just over 7 ft of water, and at low water spring tide she would just about be touching the rocky bottom at the point of the pier. With only the slightest motion on the sea, the boat would be bouncing up and down on the rocks in no time at all. In fact there was likely to be more motion at high water, but this was no better for the boat since it strained the ropes and sent *Trygg* banging and lurching against the pier. After a few sleepless nights, we decided to scuttle for shelter in Scalloway.

Meanwhile we had been finalising our plans for the bow rig, with some help and advice on the isle from crofter Rob Holbourn, a qualified if not practising naval architect. In Scalloway we were now handier for materials and expert help, and were very fortunate to meet a grand old man of Shetland, Jack Moore.

Jack at this stage was in his seventies, but still working as he had done all his life in his boat repair yard in Scalloway. He was a man of the old school—he would never charge more for a job than it was worth. When times were harder in Shetland, he used to hold up maintenance and repair bills on local fishing boats until they came in with a fine haul of fish. He knew his job backwards, and immediately took us under his wing.

He knew Foula, the Shaalds and the waters round Shetland well, and as a boy had seen the *Oceanic* on the reef. He used to say: 'I think you're crazy, but the very best of luck to you' and then go on to do all in his power to help us succeed. I remember his doing one particular job for us. We had fitted a bulky ½ ton iroko beam on to the bow of the boat, and a heavy bolt with an eye was to be driven through it. The bolt was to take a load of up to 8 or 9 tons (the secure end of the block and tackle rig) and it was vital that it held. If it broke, the whole rig would collapse with every possibility of a very nasty accident.

Jack took the bar and, working late into the evening, did a flawless job with the eye over the blacksmith's fire. We were to put colossal loads on that eye, and it stood up perfectly. On another occasion, not long after Jack had first met us, we were in the yard one weekend, racing against time to get back to the wreck before the autumn gales came in. Jack had been helping us all Saturday and in the evening turned to Alec and said: 'I don't work on a Sunday, but there are the keys to the yard. Use any tools and equipment you need. Just take a note of the materials you use.' We were virtual strangers, yet he gave us the run of the yard.

Jack retired when we were on Foula, and his business was sold to a consortium from the south. However, we came to know the workmen in the yard well, and on many occasions they were able to help out with minor repairs when we really needed them. Centralisation meant that the bills did get a bit fancy at times, though!

Work that year, 1974, progressed in fits and starts. We never had a settled spell of weather. As I look through the diary I see on occasion that we ran for Scalloway, sheltered waiting for favourable weather, returned to Foula, and two hours later were driven away again. It was a nightmare period of trying to get on with the work, only to be frustrated and driven back to Shetland. Living accommodation was almost non-existent—we always felt that a good lifting system and efficient gear was more likely to earn a few bob than a cosy bunk and plush accommodation, and made our priorities accordingly. As a result life could be a bit grim at times, when we were sheltering waiting for weather to improve.

We did get some successful lifting done, however, and we were learning all the time. We tried laying two moorings on the Shaalds so that Trygg could be held fore and aft in position, but we found that the tide would still take the boat where it wanted, and ropes would start to break and foul. So we adapted to a

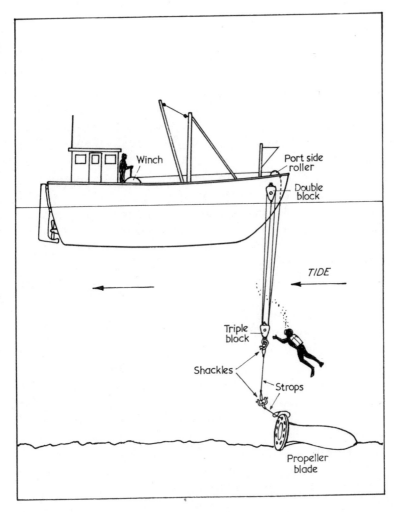

Bow lifting operations

single mooring at the bow, and the boat swivelled on it as the tide dictated.

The highlight of our year was lifting the spare propeller blades. We had the double block fitted by strops to Jack's lifting eye and hanging over the bow well above the water level. Below it was our heavy triple block, with wires carefully threaded between them. The lifting wire went on to the main drum of the winch, travelling over the bow on a specially constructed cathead and pulley wheel. Great care had to be taken in threading the blocks to avoid twisting, and we had to make matters as simple as we could for the diver, who would have problems enough with the rig anyway. Properly rigged, a 1 ton pull would lift a 6 ton load, with friction of course taking a bit from the efficiency.

The diving for these lifts was to be my job, and we had considerable problems with the first one. A mooring for the *Trygg* had to be laid uptide of the propeller blade, and the triple threaded block lowered very carefully to the seabed. If the block tipped over or accidentally went *through* the wires then the whole rig would snag unless I could manage the almost impossible job of resheaving it on the bottom—it's a hard enough task on dry land!

In addition the block, weighing well over 1 cwt, had a mind of its own on the bottom with the strength of the tide and worse, the fiendish swell, which had it leaping about like a wild giant yo-yo, battering my fingers and crashing against my body. If I had to define frustration, I can think of no better example than having a heavy block in one hand, the strop on a propeller blade in the other, and find that hauling at both there is still a gap of a couple of inches—you can't therefore shackle them together!

Eventually, after considerable effort and even more frustration, and much cursing on top and below (yes, you can swear despite the demand valve clenched between your teeth!) the blade, the strop and the block were shackled together. The signal for the lift to start was given, but still I had to hold the block in position to ensure the wires ran smoothly on the pulley wheels. This was potentially a very dangerous job as, while ensuring the wires ran freely, the diver had nonetheless to make certain that no fingers or gear got caught in the rig. We improved and almost perfected all our lifting systems over the years, but never got round this problem.

If a diver did get caught between the revolving wheels and the wires there would be no hope for him as the winchman on the boat would have no idea anything was wrong. A hand, then an arm would be dragged in, and the rest would be too horrific to think about. But it was a necessary risk, and one we thought of very carefully, and in fact all the lifting done this way was successful. Once the full load was taken up there was no danger of the wires jumping from the wheels.

When the 6 ton load was dangling a few feet below the bow, *Trygg*, now well down by the head, had to make her way back to the shallow water of the Voe before dropping the blade again. Some of the water we had to pass over was 120 ft deep, and it might have been difficult to find a brass lump dropped in error at that depth—perhaps from a broken strop. (While we were north an American carrier off Orkney had this very problem when one of their Tomcat aircraft fell over the side when they were exercising—they couldn't pinpoint the spot. They were terrified the Russians would find and raise it before them, and despite sophisticated gear only located it by hiring a trawler to drag for it!)

As an insurance against this we put a weight in a sack attached to 30 fathoms of rope with a buoy on top. If the load broke the whole sack would instantly be hurled into the water. The lift of the buoy would snake the rope from the sack and come to the surface giving an exact mark. Happily we never lost a load.

After our problems with the first blade, we thought carefully of ways to improve the system of getting the heavy block to the blade. As with the solutions to most salvage problems it was quite simple once you thought it out. The diver was first to take down a wire strop and feed it through one of the eyes on the blade. At the same time he was to take down a small light single block and tie it securely beside the blade. He then surfaced and was given the end of a light rope by the man in the boat. The diver would take this rope to the bottom, pass it through the single block and take the end to the surface again where he would tie it to the bottom of the heavy triple lifting block.

The winch drums and side barrels worked independently, so as the boatman let out the wire to run through the elongating triple block system, he was winching in the other end of the rope. This meant that the heavy unwieldy block was being winched unerringly into position, and when it was at the bottom it was immediately attached to the blade. The diver simply had to supervise, and see everything was going to plan.

It may seem complicated to the reader, but it was a most effective system which took much of the effort away from the diver and put it on to the winch systems. We were keen to try it, and the first day it succeeded perfectly. The evening before we could see that we were going to get a fine spell, but we were coming up to one of the fastest spring tides of the year. We would have to be very quick to catch the slack waters—everything would have to go like clockwork. There would be no time for delays.

Every eventuality was discussed and analysed before we went out there, and it was one of those days that we felt we were functioning perfectly as a team. As it turned out the first lift went so well that we managed to raise two blades at the next tide, and another in the evening, making a total of four for the day. Each had to be coaxed carefully back into the Voe until it grounded, and the winch was slackened off. A diver had to uncouple the load, remove the strop, and supervise the lifting of the heavy block to the surface once more.

It was exhilarating diving, with diver, boatman and boat all being stretched to their limits. I remember it being quite a struggle against a strong tide—lifting two blades on the afternoon tide inevitably meant working before and after slack water—but Alec's system worked so well it was all really automatic. The one problem that the pair of us could not solve was communication between the winchman, just in front of the wheelhouse, and the diver who had to hold on to the bow moorings or be swept away off the site. Deirdre kindly abandoned her kitchen for the day, and stood at the bow relaying messages between us.

It was a haul for the day of more than 23 tons, although the blades were not completely salvaged and there was work to be done on them still. But they were now in the sheltered waters of the Voe, and therefore much easier to work with. On each of the four lifts *Trygg* was virtually lifting her own value in metal and we had achieved it all with a total diving time on the reef of 45 minutes. We felt very pleased with ourselves, and a couple of days later we easily lifted the sixth and final loose blade.

If we thought it was going to be plain sailing from now on, the weather soon brought us back to earth with a bump. We were busy one day bringing the blades from the deep water of the Voe into the pier and under the crane—something we could do only when there was practically no motion about as the blades had to be lifted that much higher, and could damage *Trygg*'s hull if they knocked against it. Exhausted, we finished at 9 pm on a most pleasant Shetland summer evening. We went back to the Haa for a meal, and within minutes, it seemed, the weather changed. By midnight an easterly gale was blowing straight into the Voe, and *Trygg* was in serious trouble at the pier.

To take a boat the size of *Trygg* away from the pier at Foula, one had to go astern for 50 yd or so, back the boat's stern to the south side and head off hard a-starboard—just missing the north-side shallows of the Voe. In adverse weather it was a tricky operation. In darkness, as Alec had to do it, it was hair-raising! It wasn't a question of losing lives, but if one small mistake had been made the boat would have been smashed in no time. The words of many an old-timer came back to us—'You'll never manage to keep a boat that size at Foula!' As the wind howled and the white water crashed all around us, I ran from bow to stern peering for the rocks and shouting the information to the wheelhouse. We were both sweating quite a bit—both literally and metaphorically!

I nearly missed the trip, as I was throwing off the many ropes that secured *Trygg* to the pier. As the final rope was thrown on to the boat the surge pulled her clear. I had to hurl myself on to the gunwale from the pier, and just managed to grip the edge of the rail. Had I fallen in I would have had to make my own way back to the pier, for Alec could not have come back for me. I hung on grimly, as the cold, dark water was not a pleasant prospect, with the swell and the surge roaring in to the pier!

Somehow we eased our way out of the Voe in one piece, and had to dodge around at sea in the gale all night—we couldn't close on the Shetland mainland for as yet we had no radar and were travelling blind in driving rain. We were really only safe in the open sea. The conditions were so bad that for the one and only time in my life I was seasick—an occurrence that seemed to cheer up a sicker Alec considerably! It was not until first light that we were able to nose our way through the tricky channel round the isles and skerries off Scalloway.

This was to be the pattern for the rest of the summer. On occasion we would leave Scalloway in fine conditions, have a pleasant trip across to the isle, tie up—and then have to flee for shelter two or three hours later. We still managed infrequent trips out to the reef, but they were getting rarer. But in spite of this we were able to take much of the first steam condenser apart, and raised on our bow-system. We had one particularly worrying day when we lifted a 4 ton bundle of brass condenser tubes right in to the point of the pier—and then had to clear out fast when the weather worsened. We had to ensure we were back at the earliest possible moment in case a fishing boat pulled into the pier and ran straight into our load of tubes. Under the circumstances we would not have been popular!

Sensibly we now bought and fitted a second-hand radar set which meant we were no longer at the mercy of the fog. By mid-September—we have since realised that this is far too late to be considering keeping a boat at Foula—we had taken one blade to Scalloway and were returning to take one more south, and to lift 3 tons of condenser housing we had 'stored' in the relatively sheltered waters of the Voe.

It always seemed to be a race against time. We loaded our second blade, and the south-east wind that was threatening (the worst direction for Ham Voe) slowly but steadily increased. It was now the turn of the condenser housing—the final lifts of the season—and we wanted them so we could make our way south. If we ran before we lifted the housing we would have to try to come back again. Lift a 30 cwt sheet of metal over the side of a boat and you always have problems in keeping it under control. Try it when the boat is kicking about and it is potentially lethal.

One of the island lads, John Andrew Ratter, helped us with the work and it was a lively episode. I stropped the loads on the bottom while Alec and John Andrew tried to sort them out as they came up out of the water. The pendulum effect meant that the brass was swinging all over the shop and it had to be dropped firmly on the first swing—with the hope that it would not do too much damage to the deck. One of these metal sheets swinging out of control could have taken the wheelhouse off with a single blow, and the two men on deck needed no encouragement to keep out of the way. We were fortunate to escape with nothing worse than a completely destroyed gunwale on the lifting side.

The problems for Alec and me were far from over, for it was quite impossible to stow this metal below, partly because of the sea conditions but also because several sheets of the metal were too big. It is hard to think of a more awkward deck cargo, but we could do no more than lash it and support it as best we could, take the trip to Scalloway very slowly, and pray that the weather would hold for three or four hours. It was with considerable relief that we arrived in the sheltered waters of the harbour, for if the load had moved across the deck there was little or nothing we could have done about it.

Stormbound for the next few days, we cut up our sheets of brass and stored them below, taking great care to lock one piece into another to ensure they would stay solid even in heavy seas. We wanted to take a complete blade south with us, feeling that a museum or interested collector might want to buy it—the offer is still open—and the top foot of the blade stuck out of the hatch. So the hatchboards had to be cut around the blade, and we hammered down tarpaulins over the jutting-out piece of metal to keep the water out if seas broke over the deck.

We left for the trip south when the gales had moderated, but there was still a heavy sea running and we had a lumpy ride through the notorious Sumburgh Roost, where all the tidal complexities of the North Sea and the Atlantic meet and try to sort themselves out. We pushed on, despite gale warnings, and nightfall found us east of Orkney in a wicked-looking sea with a Severe Gale 9 hitting us right on the nose. We felt some of the same mixed exhilaration and fear that we had experienced in earlier days on the *Oceanic*, but fear wasn't of the unknown—its boundaries were clearly defined and real. We both knew we shouldn't be in the position we found ourselves in but, now that we were, there was no other option than to make the best of it.

It was in conditions like this that we really felt the lack of manpower, for *Trygg* had a heavy wheel, and steering even in pleasant conditions left aching arms and tired legs. The automatic bilge pump was not functioning so every half hour or so one of us had to stagger out on deck—getting absolutely drenched in the process—and work a manual pump. Occasionally one or other of us would get a few minutes rest in a sleeping bag just aft of the wheel.

Trygg was really heaving about, but seemed to be coping admirably so we were not unduly worried. But we never saw the big one that hit us. One moment we were battering through the heavy seas, the next there was a terrific crash and we seemed to stop stone dead. I was tossed effortlessly from my makeshift bunk and landed around Alec's feet. His head banged against the wheelhouse window as water poured in everywhere. *Trygg* wallowed and floundered with tons of water on her decks, momentarily totally vulnerable to another wave that would completely swamp her. But, as the water streamed from her narrow scuppers, she shook herself like a dog emerging from the water and recovered her balance. Small, fat, forgotten and even ugly she may have looked in her berth at Peterhead, but that night showed she was quite capable of regaining her former glories. *Trygg* meant so much more to us both after that night.

The wave caused damage below, too. The heavy-duty batteries

were torn from their solid casings, and tossed like discarded wrappings across the engine-room. The aft engine-room hatch was smashed in an instant by the huge weight of water, which poured like a waterfall down below. Our bilge pump was blocked, and for a while we were shipping far more water than we were pumping out.

The rest of that seemingly endless night we took it in turns to go on deck in the teeth of the gale, hanging on to what we could in order to man the pump, all the time keeping an eye out for the freak, monster wave that could sweep a man off the deck. It was back and forward, back and forward, . . . all night long.

It was the worst night we ever had at sea, but we came through it with a much happier view of what *Trygg* could stand. *Trygg*, 'safe' or 'secure' those Norwegians had called her, whether she was pushing out that little bit further for that extra haul of fish, or slinking in through the fjords giving the German invaders the slip. She was aptly named.

It is difficult to put into words those sea conditions which boats can experience so far north in Britain. Far sounder boats than *Trygg*, with much more experienced crews than we were, fairly regularly simply disappear off the face of the sea. Often we will never know what happened to them, but scarcely a year passes without at least one disaster.

The 80 ft long Aberdeen trawler *Coastal Empress* was one of the fortunate ones that lived to tell the tale. She was 16 miles south of Foula when she so nearly met her end. The wind was only force 6 or 7, and the waves about 10 or 15 ft. They saw their wave but could do nothing about it. An estimated 80 ft wave had built up out of nowhere to smash down on their vessel. A photograph of the steel casing on the wheelhouse made it look as if a bomb had gone off in it.

'There was nothing we could do but hold on,' said one of the crew of the shattered vessel. 'If there had been a second wave we would have definitely gone over. Now I know how those boys on ships which were overwhelmed must have felt.' We too had a fair idea.

At daylight we reached the Scottish mainland and pulled into Fraserburgh for temporary repairs. A fuel line had been broken in the crash, and although we had partially stopped the flow there was diesel all over the engine—and us! One of the cylinder liners had to be replaced.

We were fortunate that by chance Seaforth Engineering, the main Scottish agent for marine Kelvins, was based in that port and their top engineer had the repairs done in a few hours. He also gave Alec invaluable advice on the workings of the engine, and what he should do if he ran into trouble. Four hours later we were on our way and arrived at Tayport the next day. The record in the diary is only one word. 'Dropping!' That just about summed it up.

The season was all but over. Soon we went north again in more leisurely style on the *St Clair*, and across to Foula by the mail boat. We had four tons of condenser tubes still fastened together lying on dry land but so close to the sea that a Foula winter gale would sweep them back into the sea again. The tubes were held together by four brass plates, and each tube had to be cut free with the zipper, or the brass plate smashed with the sledgehammer. Again it was the less glamorous side of salvage but after a couple of days' work—similar, we mused, to convict labour—we had the part condenser safely in our yard. Now for next summer.

11 (*above*) Garda stack at the north end of Foula;

12 (*below*) *Trygg* carrying a total weight of about 14 tons – the propeller boss and about two tons of propeller shaft – slung over her bow. She is almost ready to sink!

13 On the sea-bed, a diver prepares the port propeller for the blasting operation. The blades are still bolted to the boss, though in the foreground one blade has started to come free (*Alec Crawford*)

5

Lifting a Liner
Piece by Piece

Although we had made several successful lifts with *Trygg*'s side-lifting systems, it was obvious that the stop-gap repairs we had made to the mast and derrick would not do in the long term. When we had the long winter break we could concentrate on getting the lifting gear just how we wanted it. The existing gear was just not up to standard for the loads and stresses we wanted to put on at the Shaalds.

The problems in designing gear to do a straight lift do not pose so many pitfalls. But on the Shaalds the boat would hardly ever be stationary, and the load being lifted would on occasion get jammed in other wreckage. A rocking and heaving boat puts massive strains on the lifting gear, so the equipment would have to be the very best.

Alec turned to his drawing board and mechanical calculations, taking into account the various problems he knew we would experience. From there we went on the long trek round the Fife scrapyards once more to find the heavy tubed steel suitable for a mast and stays, based essentially on a tripod mast system. Our main mast was once an integral part of a large sugar-beet refinery. We put a solid steel plate on the deck to spread the load and mounted the mast system on that.

Our task was made no easier by the fact that the workshop facilities we had access to were 8 miles away from *Trygg*'s sheltered berth at Tayport harbour, and heavy pieces of steel had to be carried to and fro for the trial fittings. Countless hours were spent with the welder and the burning torch, and further fittings were attached under the deck and to the side of the hull itself to spread the loads over the whole boat and make the lifting gear rock-solid. We were to have no major problems with that gear once it was completed.

During that winter we were alarmed by the fall in scrap prices for our copper and brass. The prices we received from the metal merchants were directly connected to the world commodity price of copper and, to a lesser extent, the prices of tin and zinc. The industrial nations of the world were going through a slump, the demand for metals was drastically decreased, and so the price tumbled.

Manufacture of military hardware for wars uses a lot of non-ferrous metals, and America's withdrawal from Vietnam meant a further reduction in demand and consequently a drop in the price. Furthermore, the copper producing countries, in Africa and South America for example, were unable for various reasons to get together in a cartel like the OPEC countries, and thus were unable to slow down the drop. In our early days on the *Oceanic*, back in 1974, dealers were paying about £950 a ton for scrap copper—during our final full season, 1978, they were offering well under £700 a ton, and of course the buying power of the money was much less. We just had to make up the difference by recovering that much more scrap than before!

When the price plummeted during the winter of 1974, however, we were concerned that the drop would continue below the level of economic viability even for our shoe-string operation. To hedge our bets, we spent many days making nets suitable for sprat and whitebait fishing in the river Tay, and constructing the booms and the initial gear needed on *Trygg*. Fortunately the prices never went below that critical figure, and we were able to get on with the job we really wanted to do—salvage from the *Oceanic*.

With our boat literally going from door to door we were able to ferry far more gear than before—a new water tank for the Haa, for example, doubling our water 'reservoir'; field drains to run the water from underneath the house to make the whole place drier; a mountain of tins and supplies direct from the Cash and Carry to make food ordering easier; all sorts of odds and ends, including food for the islanders. The list was seemingly endless, and *Trygg* made the trip north with almost as much weight in her as she had in a 'scrap run' going south!

We were very eager to get going again, so at the first hint of a settled spell towards the end of March we were off on the 36 hour trip north. With *Trygg*, at the start of a season, this was something of an ordeal as both the boat and the crew had been laid up for the winter and it took a while to get everything working properly. Alec's non-stop seasickness put a great strain on him—and a fair bit on me as well towards the end of a trip as exhaustion overtook me after long spells at the wheel.

I never ceased to be amazed at the courage Alec displayed with this terrible seasickness. As a youngster he had even done a mid-winter spell on a fishing boat off the north Norwegian waters, working on deck and never getting over his seasickness for the whole fortnight of the trip. He has a great love of the sea that drives him on time and again.

Despite the seasickness he is able to recover from it temporarily if an emergency occurs. *Trygg*'s fuel filters were not working efficiently, and we were not as far north as we thought when we were hit by a near gale and snow showers. The tide had taken us west, and we were not far off the island of North Ronaldsay—a real graveyard for ships if ever there was one—when the sick engine showed signs of stopping altogether. Under the shadow of the lighthouse the pair of us went down to the engine-room, where the reek of diesel fuel made even me feel queasy and must have been much worse for Alec, and solved the problem—Alec alternately giving me instructions as to what was to be done and being sick in the bilges. Yet another blow for the romantic image of the salvage diver!

The weather was far too wild to consider a landing at Foula, so we changed course and headed straight for Scalloway's sheltered harbour. No sooner had we got the ropes secured than we hopped on a bus bound for Lerwick, where apparently I caused some hilarity among our friends from Scalloway by slumping totally unconscious in a deep sleep on the shoulder of a matronly woman I had never set eyes on before! We made our way direct to the headquarters of the Royal National Mission to Deep Sea Fishermen where as usual our priorities were bath, sleep and food. Over the years the mission was to prove a real haven for us after boat trips and a spell on Foula—I never knew a bath could be such a luxury—and all the staff made us very welcome. We always had to pay the more expensive 'merchant seamen' rates, however, never successfully pressing home our argument that, literally, we were 'deeper sea' than most fishermen!

We had decided that our policy of trying to keep *Trygg* at the Foula pier was totally unsuccessful—our last-minute flights from bad weather had been all too frequent the previous year. Instead, we would lay down heavy moorings at the mouth of the Voe where, if the tackle was right, the boat would lie quite happily in weather that would be hopeless if she were at the pier. But the boat would be bobbing just a few feet from the rocks and one faulty piece of chain, or one shackle coming undone, would mean total disaster. The whole responsibility would be with us, and it *had* to be right.

Our determination to make an early start to the salvage was dented by ten days of strong winds, making a landing at Foula's exposed pier virtually impossible. What we planned to do was to make a quick crossing to the isle with *Trygg*, drop all our equipment, food, spares and miscellaneous cargo—we picked up a lot of animal feed for the crofters while in Shetland—and run back the same day to Scalloway. There we would leave the boat at a safe and sheltered mooring till the settled summer weather arrived, and by that time we would have a heavy mooring sorted out for ourselves in Ham Voe.

At the beginning of April we had a fine day, but it was only temporary and as we made our way to Foula the wireless boomed out the familiar gale warning: 'Fair Isle, southerly, six to gale eight.' We had just time to throw all the cargo on the pier, for me to jump off to attend to it, and for Kenny Gear (wanting to visit the mainland) to board as second crew before Alec had to rush out of the exposed and lively Voe. It was the old, old story. No sooner were we there than we had to rush off again.

It was at this time that we acquired a third permanent member of the diving team. John Andrew Ratter, a Foula crofter in his early 20s and married with two young children, had previously had to leave his home at Punds for spells in the summer to work on the mainland to supplement the meagre living he and his wife, Francie, managed to earn from their croft. He had helped us on occasion with boat duties the previous year, and was a fine agreeable soul to work with. He was excited at the possibility of finding work on Foula (we were to become the island's biggest employer, with one part-timer—with the exception of the county council) and he wanted us to teach him how to dive.

We weren't keen. We have always felt that if you teach someone how to dive you really have a responsibility for his diving from then on, and that the Shaalds, even though John Andrew knew them well as a boatman, was no place for a novice to learn the tricks of the trade. Without giving him an outright 'No' during the 1974 season, we hedged and tended to drop the subject. He could not swim at all well, and we felt it best to keep him out of the water.

But he really meant it, and we reckoned without his very considerable determination. That winter he had bought some neoprene and constructed himself a basic, though not very efficient diving suit. He acquired a pair of fins, a weight belt, a mask and a snorkel.

The previous year, as I have explained, we had lifted large bundles of condenser tubes into the more sheltered waters of the Voe, where we methodically lifted them aboard in smaller numbers. Inevitably, odd tubes lay scattered about the bottom in the 30 ft of water—we intended to bring three more condensers in to that spot and we would give the bottom a real clear up at the finish.

That's not how John Andrew saw it. After familiarising himself with the basics of snorkeling he made his way out 50 yd from the pier, to the position where we had dropped the tubes.

Taking a deep breath, he would swim to the bottom, locate two or three tubes, swim up with them, and fin to the pier with them in his arms. Time and again he did this till the bottom was practically clear, and 3 or 4 cwt of tubes lay safely on dry land.

He is a man of few words who doesn't show his emotions very often, and he played things low-key when we returned. 'I got these up for you,' he said off-handedly, waving an arm in the direction of the tubes. What he was *really* saying was: 'You might not think I will be able to dive, but you're wrong. What about teaching me?'

How could we refuse? I dropped him in by the pier, and he took to diving more readily than any other novice we have come across. He seemed virtually fearless and unconcerned, as he listened carefully to instructions.

It seemed a totally natural environment to him. I put a set on his back, walked him into 5 ft of water, told him to breathe through the valve in his mouth, and took his mask off. Then I instructed him to kneel in the water so he was completely submerged. The water ran up the inside of his nose, and this usually feels very unpleasant to the trainee. Usually they jump to their feet, but John Andrew was quite unmoved. If his mask came adrift on the Shaalds, or leaked—as frequently happens—we knew he could cope and wouldn't panic.

Next day we took him down to a small shallow-water wreck on the east coast of the island, the *Nordsternen*, which ran on to the rocks close to the shore in thick fog. It was a sheltered spot, with no tide to bother about, and the boat could moor right above him. He came through the test with flying colours. 'What about the Shaalds now?' he asked.

He had to wait for that. We all had to. Our efforts towards an early start were rewarded with not one day in the whole of April that we could safely dive on the reef, though we were 'at the alert' the whole time. The weather itself was not so bad—it would have been less frustrating if it had been—but the predominant south-westerlies, even when they moderated, still kept that lazy ceaseless swell rolling over the reef. To dive on that wreck we had to be ready at all times to go into operation as soon as the conditions allowed—and we had to have plenty of patience.

There was still much to do. We had to prepare our heavy moorings in the Voe. Our schooner wreck had a couple of lovely anchors, about a ½ ton each, that would do splendidly for us, though the chains with them were not strong enough for our purpose. It would have been impossible to bring a boat the size of *Trygg* into the narrow rocky clefts where the *Nordsternen* lay, to lift the anchors, but it was a simple matter to come in with the inflatable.

We detached the anchors, and raised them one at a time with a small lifting bag. This was a small canvas-rubber bag that a diver could easily carry under one arm. It was filled with water on the surface, and the diver took it down and fixed it to the anchor. The bag was then filled with air from a compressed-air cylinder, and when the lift was sufficient bag and anchor would float to the surface.

From there it was a simple matter of towing the anchor, still slung under the bag for the mile or so to the Voe, where it was dropped in a suitable position. We acquired a lot of heavy ground chain to link up the anchors, and the bag was invaluable for moving that around the bottom into the correct position.

Though our start on the real work was delayed, we had still plenty to do. We had our peats to cut, and house improvements to do. We repaired old diving suits and made new ones—most shallow-water salvage divers use neoprene wet suits as they get hacked about by the sharp wreckage, and a hole does not matter so much as it does in a watertight dry suit. Bought suits tended in those days to be a bit fancy with zips and gaps everywhere—which may look splendid on the model in the shop, but which spell 'cold' underwater. We ensured they were tight to the skin, and as warm as possible, by making them ourselves—though latterly we bought Comex wetsuits, designed for near-to-the-surface divers in the North Sea, and found them to be first class.

With business being as slack as it was, for the first time we had the opportunity of seeing more of the beauty and almost primitive ruggedness of the island. One memorable—and for me totally terrifying—day was spent with John Andrew as our guide on the cliffs on the west side (the Kame vies with lonely St Kilda as having the highest sheer cliffs in Britain).

Needless to say he took us only to the easy bits, but I still shudder when I think of some of the places he used to climb to. It is not that long ago that the Foula men—like the remote St Kildans up to their evacuation in 1930—relied on the birds and their eggs as a vital part of their diet, and were completely at home on the sheerest parts of the cliffs. This talent for balance and sure-footedness was inherited in abundance by John Andrew. I remember taking photographs of large numbers of puffins and guillemots sitting on a narrow ledge some 15 ft below us, but hundreds of feet sheer above the sea. 'Do you want some close-ups?' he asked me.

Before I realised what he meant he sprang down on the narrow ledge without a second thought. As he landed amid the flurry of birds—like a scene from Hitchcock's *The Birds*—he reached out and deftly caught one of each species. One false step and he would have hurtled to his death, but in seconds he was up the cliff again, a bird in each hand, climbing with his feet and elbows. I had my close-up.

Most of the Foula folk still have this skill on the cliffs and the story is still told of a crack Royal Naval climbing team which arrived to tackle the Kame, amid a great flurry of publicity in the national press. A destroyer lay off to the west, and the men landed by gemini. In a long and complicated operation the team almost made it to the top, and had great difficulty getting off again because the weather had worsened and the inflatables found it hard to get in to pick them up.

They were forced to abandon one rope almost at the top of the cliffs, and while the press was lauding the incredible climb and the brave rescue, a Foula man nipped round the back of the isle in his boat when the weather moderated, shinned up the cliff in bare feet, undid the rope, climbed down again, picked up the rope from the sea, and was away in the space of 20 minutes!

Another route on the west side which I would have labelled as only suitable for a Don Whillans was pointed out to me as the place an *old* man on Foula used to climb down to get limpets for fishing bait. Ships that crashed on to those terrifying cliffs in a storm—and no doubt some have—would disappear as though they had never been, leaving not a trace of their existence. For months on end, particularly in winter, no one goes near the west cliffs. I once had a memorable dive at the foot of the Kame. The cliff continues 50 or 60 ft sheer underwater, and it is an awe-inspiring sight as you surface and are faced by this towering wall of rock.

A great attraction to the islanders are useful items brought in floating by the sea—wood, mainly, but also fishing buoys, nets, ropes and barrels. Much of it is valuable to them, though the real attraction is the fun of getting it from an exposed inlet or *geo*, and of getting it before your neighbour so you can crow over it! We often used to think they were slightly crazy getting themselves soaked to the waist over a small piece of timber which would then be left to rot—but we ended up doing the same thing ourselves! All the wreck buoys we used on the *Oceanic* had been found round the banks, either by ourselves or by other islanders who gave them to us.

We were spoiled this year with not one but two cooks—Ros Bourne and Lesley Timmings, two English girls who had just graduated from their universities and who had been to Foula before. They planned to come across separately on different mail-boat trips, and their adventures relating to that boat won all our subsequent visitors the reputation of Jonahs.

Ros was the first to have her drama. Kenny Gear had been delayed in Lerwick for some reason or another, so it was nearly dark and slightly misty by the time they left for home that evening. The engine was far from reliable, so when they didn't arrive at the scheduled time there was a bit of a panic.

The west-side lifeboat was launched from Aith and we spent the night climbing round the island's rocky coastline with torches in case the boat had drifted ashore. The morning papers got hold of the incident and their first editions headlined the story 'Foula mail boat missing—with divers' cook on board'. It can't have been cheery reading for her relatives!

Actually there wasn't too much real concern on the isle as the mail boat, not in the finest of condition, frequently broke down. It wasn't too bad a night, and Jim and Ken were both experienced seamen, so we didn't fear the worst.

What had happened was that the fog had come down and for the first and only time they had failed to find the island—the boat had a compass but no other navigational aids. They didn't know whether they were north or south of Foula, and eventually had to make their way back to the Shetland mainland.

The only boat they saw was a Russian spy ship, which regularly used to lie between Foula and the Shetland mainland monitoring a communications network on the west side of Shetland, passing information, or so the locals believe, between Europe and America. Whenever a world crisis developed, like a Middle East flare-up, you could be sure the Russian would return. Alas the Foula mail-boat men were a bit shy about going up to him and asking where the island was—a pity, perhaps, because I'm sure he would have known!

There was another amusing incident concerning that same Russian. We were doing blasting work on the *Oceanic* one day, and he was perhaps 7 or 8 miles away from us. By coincidence, almost as soon as we had let off the bang he moved away. The islanders ribbed us that we had managed to chase him away, and I suppose it is possible that with their sophisticated equipment the Russians might have registered the shock waves. I somehow doubt if they were actually frightened of us, but if *The Other Titanic* reaches a Russian bookshop and is read by an Ivan with sore ears—sorry, chum!

The next week our second cook, Lesley, didn't even board the mail boat as it broke down on its way across to fetch her and the mails. Fortunately the engine spluttered to a halt soon after the boat had left the pier, and we effected the 'rescue' by inflatable, actually towing the mail boat back to shore with our tiny craft. This time the mail boat proved to be gravely sick, so for the first time our inflatable was—albeit unofficially—pressed into service as carrier and collector of Her Majesty's mails as well as itinerant cooks. Alec made a much faster trip than the mail boat would have done, and he suggested tongue-in-cheek to the Walls postmaster that he should only carry the first-class letters on such a speedy service.

Official-looking mail bags were stuffed into much less official-looking old polythene fertiliser bags to keep the correspondence dry, but no one seemed to bother about the lack of formalities. It's one of the joys of Foula. We were subsequently to make several mail/fuel/supplies runs for the island with *Trygg*.

That evening, 3 May, saw the first suitable weather for us to dive on the Shaalds. The wreck was unmarked, and we were quite pleased with ourselves that we could now read the medes so accurately that we could drop the diver on the propeller shafts first dip. We felt confident enough to put John Andrew in, though of course we kept a very close eye on him initially.

The problem often facing a novice diver is that he has had, or should have had, teaching on all the various horrible things that could happen to him—a bend, an embolism, nitrogen narcosis and so on. He *must* breathe out as he ascends, as a lungful of air taken in at 30 ft would take up twice the volume in his lungs were he to surface without exhaling, with very nasty results. An experienced diver will automatically do all the right things, but if you're not careful your novice—who is pretty anxious and excited about his dive in any case—may have so much in his head that he is not thinking *if* he is going to die, but *how*!

The trick is to keep him busy. On John Andrew's first dip he was handed a massive wrench and set to undoing some of the loosened 32 lb nuts that held the propeller blades on to the bosses. He came up three-quarters of an hour later, exhausted but elated by partial successes. He was full of the technical problems of his job—he quickly learned that you must anchor yourself firmly on the bottom for such a task or you'll just float about like a spaceman, achieving nothing. Not a word about his diving! He had subconsciously grasped immediately that the diving itself achieved nothing. It was merely a vehicle for the skills and hard work that really counted on the bottom. It was an ideal way for him to gain confidence on the seabed. But he was amazed by his first real dive, and totally enthralled by the sheer size of the engines and the propellers.

'Here you are, on our own personal wreck site, in the middle of nowhere with the beautiful backdrop of the isle rising from the sea,' I told him. 'There's no pollution, crystal-clear water— just perfect except for the bloody tide. You're the third man alive and the fourth person ever to see the wreck. Many a diver has been in the water hundreds of times and never seen anything half as spectacular as you've seen in just one dip. They'd give their eye teeth to change places with you.' He was to have many a hard dive on the wreck in the future.

With three working divers now, we employed a system whereby Alec would concentrate on the explosive operations, laying the charges, clearing the area and so on. Another diver, usually John Andrew—to give him experience and because I was the only one of the three who did not feel seasick in the moored boat as the swell rolled languidly over the reef—would be sent down to 'scrounge'. This was great fun and entailed swimming round the engines and trying to pull free small bits of brass and copper which would be lifted into the inflatable. John Andrew is tough and strong, and revelled in the work, and used to rip out some pretty impressive pieces.

The ship had a double bottom—two layers of steel with a gap between them—and a lot of the pieces we wanted used to fall down holes between them. They were usually confined spaces, with razor-sharp metal round about, and very dangerous to go into head first. It was not uncommon to see a diver take off his diving cylinder to reduce his bulk, hold the set above his head (still holding on to the breathing valve between his teeth!) and lower his legs into the hole to grab a small fitting with his feet.

Alec was busy all this time digging his holes, like some kind of marine termite. As the wide-span propellers—well over 20 ft—were almost completely buried, he decided that by far the most effective way to break them off the shaft would be to get behind and underneath them. I don't want to go into the technicalities of explosives work, but it is much easier to break off and break up a propeller when it is still attached.

Let us make a simple analogy. Take a thin bamboo stick, put one end in a vice, and you could bend and break the other end with almost no effort. But try suspending it from a thin thread. Then you could hit the stick as hard as you like without breaking it. It would just fly away.

With the propellers we were faced with exactly the same principle. We wanted to do the whole job in one, so the propeller shaft would act in the same way as the vice. The explosive charge would be met by massive resistance, the shaft would break and the boss and blades would be thrown clear.

Dive after dive Alec would go down with crowbars, a hammer and chisel, and other tunnelling gear. At the end of his dip he would let off a small charge to dig deeper. With a shovel and primitive airlift he would scoop and suck the débris clear. A gale swept it back in again, and so the clearing operations had to be redone. By the time he was finishing his task, all the other diver could see was a pair of fins sticking out of the hole, as Alec dug even deeper.

But his perseverance and patience paid off, and we were rewarded with a perfect job. With the explosives packed up hard right underneath the propellers, the full power and the sharp crack of the explosives against the resistance of the heavy shafting resulted in the 29 ton propeller sheering the shaft, with the blades breaking off like petals on a daisy. Propeller and blades were lifted clear of the stern frame and broken off into individual units. With Alfred Nobel's invention correctly applied, it was all as easy as our mythical stick in the vice.

Every care and safety precaution has to be taken, of course, whenever explosives are handled. Although they are now much safer and more stable than they used to be, we were always very strict in carrying out checks and obeying every letter of the rules. The firing cable—or det wire as we called it—was connected last thing so the tide could have least effect on it, and there was less chance of the cable cutting on wreckage. When everyone was aboard, the cable and the anchor mooring were let out so the inflatable was not over the top of the charge, though the tremendous weight of water on top of the charge means there is little or no spout from that depth, even with quite large charges.

There was always quite a moment of apprehension just before a charge was let off, because occasionally it would fail to fire—perhaps the detonator had come loose from the charge, or the det wire had got damaged or, as happened to us on just one occasion, we had a duff detonator. Then a diver, after waiting for a while, would have to go down to sort it out—a job Alec and I both loathed—for although the book said everything was safe, you always just wondered. If the bang went off when you were working with it, I don't suppose you would even hear the explosion before you woke up shaking hands with the angels!

The propeller blasting operation may seem simple enough as I describe it, but it was a very real worry to us; if the propeller had come off as one then the individual blades would have been harder to break off—a charge would simply toss the whole fitting into the air and down again, still intact.

There is a lot more to this scale of salvage operation than just picking up the shiny bits, and all the explosives work was meticulously thought out and planned. Often Alec would climb out of the water after his work deep in thought and on the journey home he wouldn't join in the banter and high spirits that usually followed a dive.

Once ashore we would pull off our suits, grab a hot cup of tea and crowd round the roaring peat fire to get back the body-heat loss. But not Alec. His mind would have been toying over some part of the wreck, machinery or fittings that he did not fully understand. Out would come his salvage 'Bible', Sothern's *Verbal Notes and Sketches for Marine Engineers*, with full details of steam engines of that period, and he would thumb through the well-worn pages till he got the answer. Only when he saw how it was put together could he decide the best way to take it apart. With that solved, he would relax again until the next piece foxed him. By the end of our operations it wasn't often we were baffled.

With this work successfully accomplished and with the summer weather becoming more settled, we had to make plans to bring *Trygg* in. We were happy with our decision to leave her at a mooring, albeit exposed from some directions, and had prepared our two anchors and chain. But as a main mooring anchor, which the boat would depend on in south-easterly weather (probably the worst for the Voe), we thought we could do a lot worse than use the *Oceanic*'s own anchor.

We relocated the *Oceanic*'s bow easily enough, but like the rest of the wreck it was extensively broken up. The ground forward was very uneven, with slabs of rocks jutting up from the bottom and gullies running off into the reef itself. Wreckage was scattered all around, tailing off down the reef into deeper water.

First we found the immensely powerful winches used for the 9 ton anchors and their heavy chains. The wheels were over 12 ft in diameter, and the teeth were made of manganese brass for extra strength against wear—these teeth were one of the final salvage jobs we did on the wreck, not in itself a very rewarding exercise, but one which gave us great satisfaction because of the difficulties we had to overcome to get them.

Nearby lay the two anchors, still in the remains of their hawser pipes. It was the impressive size of the chains which surprised us most. They were still in fine condition and we were later to discover that each link, even after being worn by age and use, weighed more than 70 lb. We decided that *Trygg* could lift the anchor, which at that time we estimated in our ignorance as about 5 or 6 tons, and 14 links of the chain.

Normally people tend to overestimate the size and weight of objects in the water, partly because a magnifying effect does indeed make things look bigger. Perhaps we overcompensated for this, because invariably we calculated items—the propeller blades, the bosses, the condensers, the anchors and so on—as being much less than they subsequently turned out to be. One of our cooks, Lesley, was an honours graduate in mathematics from Cambridge, so we shouldn't have got our sums wrong! Perhaps we gave her incorrect measurements.

Using the same block-and-tackle system as we used to lift the propeller brass, we planned to lift the anchor and fourteen links of chain and lay them on the south side of the Voe. We would then connect up the ground chains with our two schooner anchors, and lift another section of *Oceanic* chain to form the bulk of the up-and-down chain to the *Trygg* herself. It was designed to hold 30,000 tons of ship—surely it would do for our little *Trygg*.

We blew off the fourteen links of chain with difficulty—like much of our work, it's an easy job when you know how! John Andrew was entrusted with his first major lifting job—we felt it wouldn't be the end of the world if we made a mistake and dropped it on the trip home as there was always the other anchor, which we could recover if needs be. But John Andrew made a fine job of the stropping, which must have increased his confidence, and we soon had the lift on. We were surprised when *Trygg* buried her nose towards the water level. The anchor was obviously heavier than we thought, but we got it home safely.

The anchors and chains were now all in position in the Voe and our moorings were ready. It had been a lot of work preparing them, but they were to prove vital for the success of the operation as a whole, as we could relax in the moderately bad weather to prepare ourselves to take advantage of the good spells. The boat was a hundred times safer at her moorings than tied to the shallow pier.

We were also lucky on the occasions we had to leave our salvage boat at Scalloway to have the help of the harbourmaster there, Magnie Tulloch. Leaving unattended a boat the size of *Trygg* while we were at Foula, despite Scalloway's sheltered

14 Meals during salvage work were always hurried affairs. John Andrew Ratter grabs a bite while keeping watch on the winch-wire (*Colin Martin*)

15 (*above*) The *Oceanic*'s thrust block, with shoes inserted, on the wreck site. The thrust block would be in the very heart of the ship, and this picture shows how clear it was from the rest of the wreckage, and therefore just how broken up the ship was (*Alec Crawford*);

16 (*below*) a propeller blade, weighing 5 tons 17 cwt, is winched ashore by crane at Scalloway pier after *Trygg* had made the 25 miles crossing from Foula (*Robert Johnson*)

anchorage, would have been a nagging worry but Magnie—over and above the scope of his normal duties as harbourmaster—looked after the *Trygg* as if she were his own. He would regularly pump out the bilges, check moorings and ropes, and generally see that everything was in tip-top condition.

He and many other friends we made in Scalloway—like Walter Scott of TTF, a Scalloway-based shipping concern, who kept us up to date with met reports, and Robbie Johnson who supplied us with diesel—took a very close interest in our progress on the *Oceanic*. There was an attitude of mind on Shetland that we found very refreshing—people's positive willingness to help rather than a stream of negative forecasts of failure.

One such example came with the tractor, trailer and digger attachment that an islander wanted to bring across to Foula. There was no recognised way of getting this equipment across, so we said we would try to help him out. Although *Trygg* did not possess a Board of Trade load-line and strictly we shouldn't carry such a 'cargo', we realised that a Shetland official would know that we were not doing the job for profit but as a favour, that there was no other way the crofter could get vital equipment into Foula, and accordingly turn a blind eye.

All went according to plan, and after much humping and shifting the bulky and heavy equipment somehow fitted on to *Trygg's* confined decks. Everything was lashed tightly, and as there was a bit of a blow, it was decided to wait until conditions moderated.

It was at this stage that things started to go wrong. By pure chance one of the Scalloway boats was due for an inspection, and to our horror we learned that it was to be carried out by an official, noted for his strictness, from 'south'—a general term used by Shetlanders for anyone unfortunate enough to live south of Orkney. The official would be bound to see *Trygg* and her abnormal load, and would be equally certain to demand it be taken off.

John was desperate to get his equipment, so the only real answer was to put to sea. It was a very lively trip, with tractor and trailer heaving first one way and then the next, though thankfully remaining tightly lashed. A Foula landing was impossible, and it was an odd sight with *Trygg*, tractor, trailer and digger all kicking about restlessly at the mooring! They were all successfully landed when the weather moderated.

Two very welcome guests who visited us at this stage were Alec's old diving partner Peter Grosch, and his wife Grizelda. Now based in France, Peter was a diving superintendent working on one of the North Sea rigs and welcomed the chance of a 'busman's holiday' during a two-week break from the oil work. He was, and is, one of the most competent and assured divers we had ever worked with—totally at home in the environment. We had told him about the severe problems we had with the tide, but divers on any wreck tend to exaggerate this problem—particularly from the safety of a bar stool. Peter, however, had heard of the wreck being written off because of those conditions by the early Scapa Flow divers and knew it had been untouched for many years, so he suspected there was some truth in the rumours.

Knowing he could well look after himself we played a bit of a trick on Peter. We put him into the water a little early in the tide. The speed of it practically tore him limb from limb, his face mask landed up somewhere round the back of his head, and his fins were half off. He was hanging on to his demand valve with his teeth like grim death, and moments later he surfaced spluttering: 'This is bloody ridiculous!'

We ribbed him that we had waited for a nice slack tide to put him in but, taking the joke in good humour, he nonetheless was genuinely surprised by the speed of the tidal flow.

While we sat around waiting for the tide to slacken, Peter explained that divers in the North Sea were really struggling to work around the 2 knot speed, and in anything over that operators had to think of some other method of dealing with the problem. He estimated when we were working to our limits we would be around that mark, but at peak flow the tide would be much too fast for us. We were glad to have such an experienced man with us, if only to prove that our stories, and the stories of Robbie and his associates, were not wildly exaggerated.

I remember one beautiful summer evening, after we had dived on the Shaalds a couple of tides, climbing up Hamnafield to a height of about 1,000 ft. It had been a perfect day, and in the last of the shimmering heat Shetland lay spread out as a rambling backcloth while to the south, nearly 50 miles away, Fair Isle jutted out on the horizon as clear as could be. There wasn't a breath of wind and the sea was flat. As I sat down to drink in the impressive scene I half-closed my eyes, and the motionless sea almost seemed like a vast barren desert. Barren, that is, except for a narrow burn or stream bubbling through the middle of it. It was the Shaalds at full flood, with the water funnelling and accelerating over the reef. It was the most graphic display of the speed and power of the tide that I ever saw.

We took advantage of the extra hand to get the newly blown-off blades into the pier at Foula. Peter had done this type of work before, so he took to it with ease. We soon had the five blades off the reef (making an overall total of 11), though not without incident. On the first lift we did not pull the blade close enough to the hull of the *Trygg*, and the wires twisted dangerously on the way in. That called for a tricky dive to untwist the load in the open sea, and it was a mistake we weren't to repeat.

On another partially buried blade the boat was winched so far down that the top block was covered and the bow almost under the water. It was a very anxious moment as the boat was straining to her very limits. A small swell came in, put a little bit extra lift on, and the blade tore free with a terrific jerk. Alec noted briefly in the diary: 'Should have blasted it out first.' If I remember rightly, the point was made much more forcefully on deck at the time. All's well that ends well!

Peter was only with us briefly, but we enjoyed his company. John Andrew had gained a lot from working with a man so experienced and happy in the water, and Peter in turn was most impressed by John Andrew's abilities. 'I could get you a job in oil work tomorrow,' he told him, but John Andrew was never really tempted. He had his fishing, and diving work on his own doorstep, and that's what he wanted.

There was one slightly worrying aspect to the propeller blades. Had we found and located them all? Each propeller had originally had three blades, but when we first saw the starboard propeller one blade was missing. We had found five blades that were definitely spares, and one lying close to the starboard propeller which was either another spare or the blade that was knocked off at the time of the wrecking.

The propellers, of course, turned in opposite directions so that a port blade is a different shape from a starboard one. It is illogical to assume that at the time of building there were three port spares and only two starboard ones put on the boat—obviously it must have been three and three. We found and recovered a total of 11 blades. Where was the twelfth?

As we saw it there were three possibilities. First, that a blade was knocked off as the Oceanic first slipped on to the reef, perhaps some distance from the place where the wreck finally broke up. Second, we had missed seeing a spare blade from the area we had recovered the others—perhaps it was buried in other wreckage. Or third, there were only five spares on the ship when she went aground.

We gave the matter a good deal of thought, and searched all round the area for the missing 6 ton lump of brass—nearly £4,000 scrap value at the bumper 1974 prices. Our searches were not entirely in vain, for although we found no blade in those remote spots we did find scattered all around some other valuable smaller pieces of metal which we might otherwise have missed. The final answer to the question came in the most unexpected manner.

Way back in 1902 a pretty 18-year-old girl was thrilled by her first trip in the mighty Oceanic. Although she was travelling on the £20 steerage fare, she was able to enjoy the concert room and 'silent' cinema, and even played the piano on deck for dancing. The ship had left Liverpool en route for New York the day before. At 3 am the following day, while the passengers slept, the ship suddenly gave a great shudder, and the throbbing engines fell silent.

In no time at all the passengers were summoned on deck by the stewards, and the ship's lifeboats were lowered over the side. One of the crewmen was a diver, and he was sent over the stern to see where the damage had occurred. The captain, 'a fine-looking chap, with a short beard, who looked lovely in his uniform' in the eyes of his teenage passenger, anxiously waited for his diver's report. The bolts in one of the propeller blades had come loose, and the blade had been thrown off. The turning motion of the propeller, however, had spun the 6 ton lump of metal into the hull of the ship and made a considerable hole. But the pumps were equal to the problem, and the diver reported that the ship could carry on carefully on one engine, although they would be two days late in New York.

Seventy-five years later the pretty teenager was a bright 94-year-old. Mrs Beatrice Blewett, of Scunthorpe, read a small paragraph in her newspaper about salvage work on the ship she had sailed in so long ago. She wrote a letter about her experiences to a women's magazine, and from that I eventually got in touch with her. She told me:

> I remember the incident well. The lifeboats were put over the side as a precaution, and they bobbed like corks in the water. But we didn't have to use them.
>
> We were just off Queenstown on the Irish coast. I was excited and thrilled, you know. I wanted to see some excitement. I remember an old Welsh lady was very frightened, and I tried to calm her down. I told her the ship wouldn't go down. She was too big!

And that was the simple answer to our worries about the spare blade. It was not lying somewhere around the Shaalds, but had been cast off years before near the Irish coast, where it still lies. A spare would have been put on the propeller when the *Oceanic* arrived at New York and would not be replaced, since it would be very expensive to cast a single blade and there were two more spares. It was pure coincidence that we solved the mystery.

Mrs Blewett sailed all over the world on many liners, but treasures those particular memories of the *Oceanic*. She has a painting of the ship, and was delighted when we sent her a copper plate from one of the generators on the wreck—her family had it specially engraved with the *Oceanic* tale. Although she had not been well, she took the trouble to talk into a tape recorder and tell me all about her experiences. A grand old lady!

Our real lifting problem came not with the blades or the anchor, but with the propeller bosses. Each still had a 4 or 5 ft section of steel propeller shaft tapered and keyed into it, and we knew the brass alone was very heavy (we subsequently worked out, more accurately, that with its shaft each boss weighed about 14 tons, though once again we didn't suspect at the time they were nearly as heavy as that).

It was a pretty calm day, and I was just about ready to get into the water when Alec casually remarked: 'Let's try a strop in one of the bosses and put the block on it. I don't think we'll be able to lift it but we'll give it a try!' I didn't think we had a hope of lifting the boss by that means, but we had no other real ideas and I felt there would be no harm in trying.

In moments the lift was coupled up and I gave the signal to heave up and swam a few feet away to watch. The wires quivered and became bar tight, but the huge lump showed no sign of movement. And then, bump, bump, bump, it just started moving with the very slight swell.

What a fright I got when I came to the surface. *Trygg* seemed to be standing on her head, at a crazy angle! Alec had his full weight on a heavy pair of stilsons, straining at every sinew to tighten the winch belt and get a little more grip. Sweat—from the concentration, worry and effort—leapt from his brow.

Hurling off my diving gear, I jumped aboard, where the wires and blocks were making a ghastly creaking and groaning noise at the bow. *Trygg*'s sturdy frames seemed to be stretched to their limits. Water poured in like a tapstream from a hole in the stem normally high above the waterline but pulled under by the excessive weight. The bilge pumps in the engine-room would not work, as the permanent slant of the boat meant all the bilge water ran to the bow—and the more the water ran in, the heavier the weight in the bow became. John Andrew, myself, and young Davy Gear (Kenny's boy) were baling hectically with buckets.

We didn't lift the bosses more than a few feet, and literally bounced them off the reef. We knew precisely the lie of the land round the props, and by steaming the *Trygg* carefully over the shallow ground we knew so well we were able to bounce each boss in turn—like a ball tossed by the slight swell—until we moved into deeper water. It was 'action stations' all the way, and our progress wasn't made any easier by the fact *Trygg*'s own propeller was half out the water, such was the angle of the boat. The inflatable buzzed round as cover in case the *Trygg* flipped over—a very real fear. We reckoned if another boat passed close by us at speed, the wake might have been sufficient to put us down. With great care we ran into the Voe until the load grounded.

Looking back on those two operations, they were probably the greatest risk we ever took with *Trygg* during all our activities. Lifting bags would have been inappropriate and uncontrollable in such tidal conditions, and we decided it was the only way we could manage the job. Certainly it was a big risk, but most of the really stimulating salvage attempts usually are. Each boss, worth about £8,000 at the time, was more valuable than the boat, so they were risks we had no qualms about taking. We certainly couldn't just leave them on the Shaalds!

6

Island Wedding

By now we had settled into a routine and were working well as a team. Alec continued to concentrate on his blasting work, while John Andrew and I took it in turns to scrounge for the small fittings. We undertook a bit of work-study on all this, and hit on a more efficient way of lifting these smaller pieces. We acquired a few old 45 gal tar barrels and cut them in half with the zipper. Holes were cut in the sides by the razor-sharp rim, where a wire strop would be threaded through. Small holes were also punched in the bottom of the bin, so that the water inside would drain out as it was lifted aboard.

We managed to put two or three of these prepared half-bins into the gemini when we went out to the wreck and the 'scrounging' diver would drop down the mooring rope with them, one at a time, and take them to predetermined points on the site. These were then filled with scrap and left down there until *Trygg* was brought in for lifting—then the operating diver would thread a wire strop through the bin and back through itself, locking the whole thing tight, and perhaps 3 or 4 cwt of loose scrap could be lifted at once.

We could only manage this system on a place like Foula—anywhere else rival divers might appear at any moment and you would not only be leaving them loose scrap, but conveniently parcelled scrap as well! For speed of lifting we tried dropping the bins with the steel-wire strops already in them, but if the bin was left below with the scrap in it for several days (as frequently happened) the electrolytic action between the brass and the strop was so rapid that in no time at all the diver could take the strop—with a breaking strain of several tons—and pull it apart with his hands.

Copper pipes and the larger valves would not fit into the bins, but these were easily bundled with either wire or rope strops. Rope was much easier to work with, but was much more liable to rub through, weaken and break on sharp wreckage. We liked to use the rope strops particularly on days of marginal weather, when there was a fair bit of surge on the reef. This meant that if a big swell came in and the lift was not clear then the system would break at the weakest point—the rope strop—as the over-load came on.

A wire strop might hold fast and damage the main lifting gear on the boat. Breaking strops in the middle of a lifting operation could also be dangerous to the diver, but he soon learned to keep out of the way once he had given the 'up' signal!

It was about this time that we had the only two serious and potentially dangerous incidents in the water—both during 1976—during our years on the Shaalds. We had frequent cases of cut and crushed fingers and hands, a couple of minor breaks, which was only to be expected with work on such a location, but Alec's first injury was the nearest we had to a diving fatality.

Alec and I were diving together, quite close to one another but in different parts of the wreck. While I was 'scrounging' he was laying explosive charges, and working with Cordtex.

This is how Cordtex works. A diver might want to let off an explosives charge in perhaps seven or eight, or even more, separate parts of the wreck at the one time. The charge is detonated via a cable and an electric detonator after everyone is safely in the boat, and if the diver wants to put off several small charges he joins them together with Cordtex.

On the shore Alec would cut a length of this material, which looks just like a thin, white, waterproof washing line, but contains a core of powdered explosive. Before taking it underwater, he sealed both ends to keep it absolutely watertight.

On the bottom the Cordtex could be threaded through the various charges, and the detonator attached to one end. When the detonator was set off, the Cordtex would burn and explode rather like the gunpowder trail in films, though much faster (something like 21,000 ft per sec, which, when you are talking about 30 or 40 ft, is as near instantaneous as dammit!). As each separate charge was reached it would be set off—a very efficient way of working.

One of the major problems facing Alec was that he had to ensure, in difficult conditions, that the Cordtex did not get even slightly nicked or cut. It wasn't dangerous if this happened, but if water seeped into the Cordtex, then the line of detonation wouldn't pass that point, and half your charges wouldn't go off. This meant the work had to be repeated next time, everyone got very cross, and progress was slowed up.

Surge was the worst problem, and if you weren't careful your Cordtex was flapping around like a washing line in a breeze. If it rubbed against wreckage it would certainly puncture. So on this occasion, he told us later, he was laying his Cordtex with the utmost care.

It was one of those days when you needed another pair of arms and legs. I had my legs wrapped round a steel shaft, and was working with the Cordtex with both hands, trying to hang on to wreckage as well with my elbows outstretched. I was concentrating on not damaging the Cordtex, but the surge was trying to throw me all over the place.

A big wave must have gone over the top for I was suddenly wrenched free and tossed, completely out of control, into heavy and sharp wreckage. I was stunned, half unconscious, and not too sure what was going on!

He surfaced all right, but looked less than healthy. A steel spike had run through his neoprene hood and punctured the top of his head. Blood was running from it and he had a violent headache. He wanted to see his charge detonate before he let us know the full extent of his injuries—and the whole lot went off perfectly (no damaged Cordtex!)—but we could see that all was not well. We whipped him back to the island as quickly as possible where Maggie Prytheric, the island nurse, diagnosed slight concussion. He was prevented from diving for a couple of days but it could have been a lot worse. There are safer places to get concussed than out on the Shaalds on your own, in a heavy surge.

The other incident, not nearly so serious as no one got hurt, involved me and a net. Now nets, wrecks and divers certainly don't go together, but we were working on yet another system of raising several smaller pieces of brass in one lift. The net was carefully folded on the surface, put into my arms, and I swam down to a nice clear bit of wreckage. Very carefully—for of course net floats upwards when it is freed—I unfolded it a piece at a time, putting a lump of scrap on each corner until the net was spread wide. I then filled it with loose scrap, brought the corners together, and threaded a rope strop through the lot. She was ready to lift.

When I gave the signal to lift, I had to hold on to the bundle till the last moment so the boat would be on top of it and we would get a straight lift—if the net got among the main wreckage it would be in tatters in moments. I managed successfully, and as it lifted the *Trygg* drifted back on the tide. So far so good.

When I was sure it was clear, and no longer above me, I burrowed into a hole in the main engines ferreting for some more recoveries I could put up on the winch. After a few moments I wriggled my way out, and the first thing I came across, a few feet away, was my net full of scrap. 'That's funny,' I stupidly thought to myself, 'I thought I'd just sent that up.' Then the truth dawned.

The netful of scrap had come clear of the water and was just going over the gunwale when the strop broke—and the whole thing crashed down again. I thought I was well clear should such an accident happen, but I was so engrossed with my wrestling in the engine that I never heard it fall. It was a close miss, for a ½ ton of scrap falling through the water on to a diver would have been very serious.

John Andrew was making some good finds as well. When he announced he had come across a nice valve near the stern, we slightly patronisingly felt, 'The lad's found a small lump that would look fine on the mantelpiece.' When he stropped it and put it up on the winch we realised it would have to be some mantelpiece, for his high-quality gunmetal intake valve weighed ¾ ton if it weighed an ounce!

One of the problems we never satisfactorily overcame was laying efficient permanent moorings for the salvage boat on the Shaalds. With the weight of the boat, combined with the effects of tide, surge and swell, we had to use a heavy tiger rope to fix the boat to the wreck. We could not leave this rope in place permanently for the strong tide at its peak would grip the relatively wide surface area and drag it down, where it would foul and be destroyed by the motion on sharp pieces of wreckage—we know, we tried!

As a result, each time we went out to lift, the inflatable, usually manned by John Andrew, had to go in with a diver (usually myself) to lay the mooring before the salvage boat came in. This was really hard work for the diver—remember this operation had to be carried out in as fast-flowing water as we could manage, as we wanted to get on with the lifting the moment the tide slackened sufficiently—who had to pull himself physically across the wreckage into the teeth of the tide with the added drag of the heavy rope. It used to feel like a ton weight!

Eventually, as we became more proficient, John Andrew was able to make an accurate guess as to precisely which part of the wreck we were over, and the diver would hurl himself over the side and swim for the bottom as quickly as possible before the tide took effect. But if he missed his spot, he had to surface immediately, disappearing off down the Shaalds all the time, pull in the rope, get hauled aboard, regain his breath—and try again! When the tide was over—and the tide was belting in the other direction—the diver had to free the rope before he came aboard.

Looking back on it, we didn't approach our salvage work from a purely financial point of view. Sure, we wanted to do well from the enterprise, and we did, but to achieve an efficient and as near complete a salvage job as possible was also important to us for our own personal reasons. With a mixture of luck and application, we had been presented with the unique opportunity of our own 'personal' wreck—and what a wreck—and it was always important to us that we did the best possible job.

For example, a solely commercial concern would not have spent the time we did in recovering the four main four-pole generators (100 volt, 600 amps) and made, we discovered from the brass nameplate, by W.H. Allen & Son of London and Bedford. We blew the field coils off, and lifted them separately from the armatures—there were four field coils to each armature. There was seemingly endless breaking-up, cutting and cleaning work to do, but we were rewarded with about a ton of the finest quality copper from each generator. Once the copper had been cut free we had to dump the steel casings back in the sea—overall a lot of work, but an achievement that gave us immense satisfaction.

Similarly, from the financial point of view we might have gained better and quicker returns than from our labours on the tailshafts and sterntubes. The sterntube is a heavy gunmetal fitting where the propeller shaft comes out of the stern of a ship. Inside it runs a brass collar, or tailshaft, which is sweated tightly on to the last bit of propeller shafting. The brass and gunmetal are carefully machined to ensure seawater does not leak between them, and lignum vitae strips of wood (we recovered several of them) were used to help the seal.

These tightly constructed cylinders, made of non-ferrous metal, had to be ripped apart with a 'tin-opener' effect—a tiny charge was placed under the edge, set off, and this was repeated time after time until the whole length had been torn open. Again it was time-consuming for us, but we were improving on a method we had originally learned from my old colleague Chris Oldfield. We acquired several tons of top-quality metal as a bonus, and will make a much better job of it next time. Incidentally, on all the steamship wrecks Alec and I have examined—we did a rough count once, and the number was somewhere between fifty and sixty—not once did we come across a wreck that had its tailshaft liner removed. Usually propellers, condensers, all loose scrap and sometimes bearings were gone, but time after time—even on wrecks regularly dived on—several hundred pounds of tailshaft liner would remain.

The thrust blocks were probably our most exciting recoveries, and here I tell a story against myself. The 29 ton propeller drove the ship forward and this force had to be transferred from the shafting to the body of the ship. The thrust is used to transmit these forces—otherwise the engine crankshaft would soon be broken. The thrust block is used to absorb these strains. Horseshoe-type slabs are slotted into grooves for the absorption, and these are lined with whitemetal. The whole unit is held together by solid-brass pins.

To the eye of a diver who is not an engineer they look nothing special (judge for yourself on page 140). So when Alec mentioned them in discussion with me, I said firmly: 'We would have to spend a lot of time on them, and the recoveries would probably only just pay for the price of the explosives. Let's try somewhere else.'

Alec persisted. He suspected they could be quite valuable, though he never dreamed of their full worth. The whitemetal turned out to be 84 per cent tin, 10 per cent antimony and the rest copper—a very valuable metal indeed at present-day market values. And there was much of it. The thrusts I said we should 'just leave' yielded us more profit than we could have made on a 29 ton propeller. Thank heavens for Alec's library on old steam-engines!

When the boat had a full load—we used to aim for around the 20 ton mark—we would set off for Tayport, the market and a celebration. We would often top-up the load from the large sheets of brass we had taken into the Voe on the bow lift, and it was sorting out these lumps that was the most dangerous job of all. *Trygg* had a fairly small hold opening, and often lumps weighing nearly a ton had to be swung into the wings by two men in the hold, while the third had to lower the weight quickly when they were in position. It called for considerable strength, daring and agility, for one slip and someone would have been badly crushed. I still wince when I think of some of the risks that were taken.

The condenser tubes—and we handled so many thousand from the *Oceanic* that we got quite sick of the sight of them—had to be broken from their centre and end plates. As they were 14 ft long they would not fit into the hold, so they had to be laid aft on the deck. Carrying deck cargo is always to be avoided in case you run into bad conditions but—as with so many of the problems we faced—there was no real alternative.

Sometimes, if we were enjoying a settled spell in mid-summer, we would be tempted to load her really heavily. On one trip we arrived in Tayport, with just an inch or two of freeboard, proud as punch of our bumper haul. Some friends were anxious when they saw the boat pull into the river, thinking we were taking in water and sinking, but it was just another occasion when we were asking that splendid little boat to go to her limits absolutely full of scrap!

Often we would be helped on deck by some of the young islanders or ex-islanders—Andrew and Magnie Ratter put in some hard work on our behalf for the fun of a run south. Young Davy Gear and his brother Bobby, of Mogle, on occasion came out to the reef to help us, and many other islanders assisted when need be.

Andrew and Magnie are the sons of Peter and Bessie Ratter, both Foula born, who left their native island when their sons—including Jim, their eldest—came up to secondary-school age and would soon be looking for trades. Because of their close Foula connections and also the warmth of their welcome and hospitality, Peter and Bessie tend to be the base for any Foula person waiting for an opportunity, or good weather, to get back to the isle. Many was the time when we were stuck in Scalloway that Peter and Bessie made a boring stay enjoyable by throwing their home open to us. Of all the very good friends we made in Shetland, there are none we are more indebted to.

Magnie, on the surface as docile a fellow as you are ever likely to meet, nonetheless had a streak of Viking blood in him. As a youngster, about to leave school, he would never exactly run away from a fight and on a metal run south he used to beg us, while in port, to give him 'brass guard' spells. 'If I hear someone coming for the scrap in the middle of the night, I'll fix them,' he used to say with happy anticipation. Although it was rumoured that every rough 'scrappie' in the area used to nose about when our boat load arrived, the sight of Magnie, with his flowing fair hair, quizzical smile and massive shoulders, ensured we had no nocturnal visitors. We were delighted about this—I suspect Magnie was slightly disappointed!

I think unloading the scrap from the boat, and loading the lorry, was the task we found the worst chore of all. We had already handled it at least twice—once on the bottom and once stowing it below. Tayport had the disadvantage of quite substantial rise and fall of tides, so unloading could only be carried out efficiently around high water. Our derrick couldn't reach very high, so overall the unloading could take a long time. The lorry too had to be carefully loaded as scrap comes in all shapes and sizes and the metal pieces had to be locked together to ensure no movement during transit. And, of course, it had to be watched every inch of the way.

Despite being very isolated on Foula, we did see quite a lot of the west-side Shetland fishing fleet during the height of the summer. Latterly the most frequent visitor to the pier was Scalloway's *Alis Wood*, skippered by a colourful character, Alfie Jamieson, who knew the trawling grounds round Foula as well as anyone. Like fishermen everywhere, he would cannily underestimate his catches when speaking by radio to rival skippers, to prevent competition. 'How are you doing at Foula then, Alfie?' they would enquire, and he would reply: 'No very weel ava'. Just twa-three boxes.' Meanwhile crew members Hunter, Alwyn and Alan were feverishly gutting a mountain of fresh, fat Foula jumbo haddocks!

Other fishermen friends included those from the *Provider*, resplendent in Scalloway football colours. She was skippered by Bruce Watt, who along with his crew helped us in any way

17 (*left*) Tubes from the condenser just breaking the surface. Note the diver really struggling against the fast-flowing tide, and being dragged with a rope from the boat to the bow mooring where he can hang on till the load is safely stowed;

18 (*below*) the author (*left*), his partner Alec Crawford (*right*), and the third member of the salvage team, John Andrew Ratter of Foula (*centre*), discuss various salvage problems over a cup of tea, just before changing to go out to the Shaalds. Alec is working on one of the Bauer compressors which served so well during their time on Foula (*Alison McLeay*)

19 Ham Voe from the air. *Valorous* rides at her moorings, while part of one side of *Trygg*, all that remained after the wrecking, lies just below the bridge. The large lumps of propeller brass had to be taken under the bow to the point of the pier on the left, and then dragged under the crane on the right. *Valorous* had to go *inside* the pier on the highest tides, to enable the crane to lower the brass into the hold

they could. The *Provider* unfortunately sank one winter in Yell Sound, though mercifully with no loss of life. Early in the season we used to see a lot of the lobster boats—*Spray* (skippered by Bruce's father Jerry) and *Pilot Us*, with three enterprising Watt brothers, Ninky, Dodo and Pinder. Each year they used to risk their gear, their boats, and their necks way out by Foula, far from Scalloway's shelter.

For many years the Shaalds was hardly fished for lobsters, but in the 1960s word got out of its potential. Other fishing was poor at the time, and it seemed that every creel in Shetland was dug out of store and dropped on the reef.

Amazing though this may seem, islanders still tell of how 11,000 lobsters were taken off the reef in a single week, as boats dodged to and fro to avoid each other's leader lines. Of course it couldn't stand such overfishing for long, and now only the *Juna*, a lovely little boat from Skeld with Ian Gray and Malcolm Robertson, comes from the Shetland mainland. From the island itself Kenny Gear and his boy Davy fish a few creels each year, and now we have gone John Andrew has bought a boat and with former Merseysider Sam Davies (now happily settled on the isle) is trying to make a living from the lobsters.

Shetland fishermen used to think we would have to battle our way through armies of lobsters to get to the wreck, but it was never like that. Lobsters like to hide when they are not feeding, and there is no better hiding place than a broken-up shipwreck. I don't suppose we saw more than ten all the time we were on the site.

Incidentally it was an unspoken rule with us that we never sold lobster—it would scarcely have been worth our while and it could, quite understandably, cause resentment among fishermen. We would give away the occasional lobster we picked up, jokingly insisting that the fishermen give us any brass they might 'catch' in their creels. If it looks as if we might have come out worst in the deal, let me say we were in receipt of many more kindnesses from Shetland fishermen than we gave—and many a wreck site has been pointed out to us by a fisherman!

Another regular seaborne summer visitor was Robbie Shearer on the small County cargo boat *Spes Clara*. Robbie used to bring in road mending materials, small machinery, fence posts, wire, fuel and food—the list is endless. The boat was a popular visitor to the isle, and there was always a bit of a party when she arrived. The celebrations for the incoming workmen used to start long before they reached Foula—I remember following the *Spes Clara* into the pier one day and it was rather like a paper-chase. Dotted and bobbing astern seemed an endless stream of bright-red beer cans, to the accompaniment of laughs, shouts and general merry-making on board!

We also saw the occasional determined small yacht and indeed, while on Fair Isle for a quick visit, we met up with Richard Fresson, a Fife neighbour of ours, who with friends had brought *Aiva II* into northern waters. Another colourful yacht that anchored in the Voe was commanded by a large bearded Dutchman who, according to one of his companions, was a leading surgeon in his country.

I was gossiping with our next-door neighbour, Elizabeth Holbourn, about the visitors when she immediately had an idea. 'Would he look at my sick lamb?'

Elizabeth doesn't have quite so many sheep as she used to, but has a great affection for them and many is the 'caddy' or hand-reared lamb you see bounding about the floor of the Ham each spring. Some of the Foula ways with sheep are unusual—it is not uncommon to see an ailing lamb bound up in an old Fair Isle patterned jersey to protect it from the cold! Improvisation is vital so far away from professional help.

Elizabeth's lamb had a badly dislocated shoulder, and a vet's trip would cost far more than the lamb was worth. But what about the surgeon? If he can fix people, surely he can do something for the lamb. So the distinguished surgeon—who will no doubt dine out on the tale at medical dinners for years to come—made his way up to the croft house. By way of preparation he asked Elizabeth to pass down a joint of dried lamb which he saw hanging in the main room. Carefully he dissected it to see how it functioned. Having worked it out, he gently manipulated the dislocated shoulder back into position, saving the lamb's life. His fee for an operation on a human would be very substantial indeed. His reward for his most unusual 'operation' was a cup of steaming tea and fresh-baked Ham bread! He was delighted.

Another floating visitor we used to see around the Foula shores was the Fishery Protection cruiser. It was, shall we say, not unknown for fishermen to try a quick drag on the sandy bottom of the Ham—inside the limits. Usually we heard about the cruiser before she arrived, for her whereabouts tended to be a regular part of the gossip between trawler skippers on their radios. They spoke about her in their own sort of code, so the cruiser itself didn't know that they knew where she was!

Some clever cat-and-mouse tactics used to be enacted before our very eyes. I remember one fine summer day the *Provider* was hanging about the Ham, just waiting for the opportunity to shoot her nets. The cruiser hovered around, before making to the south of the island and then west to the open sea.

The *Provider* nipped down to the south end, close to the land, till she could see the cruiser moving well away. Back she came and shot her nets. But the cruiser was too clever that time and hared back, making the trawler crew haul for dear life to get her nets in. As often happens, the cruiser just went round the trawler a couple of times, saw her make for home, and let her off with an 'unofficial' warning. It's the foreigners they're really after. Nimrod aircraft help with the surveys, and now their strike force is increased with helicopters speedily moving in for arrests.

I heard a nice story the other day of a helicopter and a Shetland boat working on the east side. The Shetlander was poaching, and was heaving in his nets just as the helicopter approached. Fishermen really have to be caught in the act for a prosecution to stick, and this was a marginal case.

The fishermen were nonchalantly trying to ignore the hovering helicopter, as if to show their innocence by their unconcern. They were just waiting for the boarding party, and out of the corner of their eyes saw the lifting wire being prepared. Attached to the wire when it came down was not a naval officer but an empty fish basket! This was ceremoniously filled up to the brim by the fishermen, and the helicopter flew off without a word being exchanged. It was a good-natured way of giving a friendly warning, and ensuring a pleasant supper!

Away from the salvage, we were also involved in improvements to *Trygg*. We replaced her heavy wooden rudder—so hard to steer with on a long trip—with a steel one which we all helped to build and fit. Special bearings had to be made for it, but we provided the metal. The lathe operator really appreciated the quality of the brass—it had once been the port-engine main air-pump shaft on the *Oceanic*!

The underside wooden planking on the boat had inevitably been damaged by the large lumps of brass we had been lifting inboard on the Shaalds, often when there was motion. We double-sheathed the starboard side just forward of the wheelhouse (the side we always lifted on) and reinforced the relevant part of the gunwale with heavy plastic sheeting. Rudimentary bunks were made, with Peter Grosch's assistance, and life below became not quite so uncomfortable.

Work became especially hectic around the middle of August 1976. We were rushing to complete our final loading before the good weather broke up. John Andrew, who had worked with us so successfully that year, had to carry out repairs to his croft-house roof before he could sail south with us. We were stretched to the limit when, while Alec and I were shifting a large lump of brass casing, his finger caught between the brass and the deck. We both heard the crack.

Maggie, the nurse, looked at it and decided the bone wasn't displaced, but nonetheless tied him up in a huge bandage. 'I would normally just put a light piece of tape on the finger,' she told me afterwards, 'and tell the patient not to work. But that would be useless with Alec, so I thought a bulky bandage might make it *difficult* for him to work.'

I had the diving to do, and while Alec could rush around directing operations he couldn't work the winch with only one hand. Fortunately Moya Gerrard, a teenage girl from Lewis who had visited Foula the previous year and came back to look after our feeding operations, showed great versatility in working the winch in the difficult operation of hauling the big recoveries aboard.

We returned to the island when we had *Trygg* safely in her winter berth at Tayport, and managed to get some preparation work done for the following season. The other big event was the island's first home-based wedding since the 1940s, when Alec and Moya decided to get married on Foula itself.

It was a busy time for Moya. In addition to feeding three working divers, she had to make her own wedding dress on the old treadle machine we had in the Haa. She had to prepare the food for the party after the wedding, all baked in our tiny Calor gas oven, and kindly put in her generator-driven deep freeze by Pat Smith at nearby Leraback.

Many small things that are easily enough dealt with in modern wedding preparations were so much harder on Foula by virtue of its isolation. The minister insisted on the traditional little pep-talk to bride and groom some time before the wedding, but he was across in the Shetland mainland. The agreed day arrived with slightly overcast weather, with a gale forecast for later in the afternoon. Alec, having got this far, was not to be deflected and, despite the weather, he poured his (if I remember rightly, slightly protesting) bride-to-be into oilskins and a lifejacket and the couple bounced off into the choppy seas in the inflatable. The talk was short and to-the-point, and the pair of them were back after their 36 mile sea journey—complete with mail, fresh bread, and sound advice—by 10.30 am, happily before the gale.

Other plans had to be made. Harry had to post the banns at the post office, and get on the phone to Lerwick for special wedding telegram forms. The church had no recognised organist, but Bobby Isbister is one of the most versatile musicians on the isle. Now nearly eighty he can not only play the fiddle with great feeling, but in all probability he will also have composed the tune and be playing it on one of the many fiddles he has made himself. Bobby agreed to play the organ at the service.

The mice had got at the church organ so it didn't play, so we had to arrange to transport Bobby's organ from South Biggins in our battered old van, which had long before been scrapped in Fife and had come up to Foula on the deck of *Trygg*. Relations of both Alec and Moya had made the long trip north, and were billeted in various croft houses around the isle. Arrangements had to be made to fly the minister to and from the service by Loganair's Islander aircraft, though one island wag suggested if he was really up to the job he would walk across.

Plane loads came across from Shetland for the wedding, and more than sixty folk packed the tiny church—by far its biggest congregation for years. As best man, by island tradition it was my job to go round each house officially to 'bid' the folk to the wedding—John Holbourn and Isobel Gear from Mucklegrind; Rob and Ann Holbourn and their two bairns from Burns; Mima Gear from Mogle, the last present-day islander to be married on Foula more than 40 years before, her son Kenny, and his boys Davy, Bobby and Kenneth; Harry Gear from the post office; Elizabeth Holbourn from Ham and the two old folk she looked after, Tom Umphray and Joanne Robertson; Sam Davies and his wife Annette making a new life for themselves in the old shop building; John and Pat Smith at Leraback, other newcomers to the isle; nurse Maggie and her husband Dal Prytheric; Jim and Sheila Gear of Magdala and their children, Ross, Kevin and Penny; John Andrew and his wife Francie, and their two young daughters, from Punds; Edith Gray of Dykes; John Andrew's folks, Jock and Jessie of North Biggins; Bobby and Aggie Jean Isbister of South Biggins, their son Eric, and Katie Manson, now well into her nineties, who lives with them now, and Bessie and Walter Ratter who were visiting their old island home.

It was a delightfully informal wedding. The timing was a bit awry, Foula style, and the bride had to wait at the church for half an hour before the last plane load of guests arrived, but nobody seemed to mind. Pilot Ian Ray parked his plane outside the church and came into the service.

As the new Mrs Crawford walked down the isle she gave her bouquet to old Joanne, who was so thrilled she could hardly speak—Joanne who for so many years had been the widow of Robbie, the only other man to dive on the *Oceanic*, more than fifty years before. She was our next-door neighbour, as sweet and as kind an old lady as you could hope to meet, and especially close to Moya.

Shotguns were fired as the couple emerged from the church (a Shetland custom to frighten away evil spirits), and everyone walked down in procession to the schoolroom, which had been converted into a reception room. After the toasts the dancing began—with the 'Shaalds o' Foula', what else?—and continued right through the night.

Like our salvage plans, the wedding was dependent on the weather. Fog would mean no plane, no minister and no wedding, but we were fortunate to get as good a day as you can expect in Shetland come September—with even enough swell on the Shaalds to make diving impossible and thus leave Alec, never really happy when good diving weather was missed, with a clear conscience!

7

The End of *Trygg*

Our bumper year was to be 1977. We had managed much preparation work in the late part of the previous year, after we had taken *Trygg* back to the safety of Tayport. All the work we had achieved in the previous years had contributed to the favourable position we were in—we had conducted our salvage operations methodically, and now we would be rewarded with some of the plum recoveries. Several of the bigger lumps were ready to come up immediately, while we had 'stored' several valves and small pumps in various holes and covered them with other wreckage—the power of the ferocious winter seas would move them otherwise.

We were getting clear of the condensers—big, valuable, but very vulnerable to being buried by collapsing engines. Now they were nearly gone, we felt we could recover more loads than ever. We used to banter with some of the fishermen about who was getting the best catch—haddocks or brass—but we were only there for a limited period, we pointed out, as sadly brass doesn't breed! There was truth behind the jest, for in any salvage operation of our type, the easiest and most accessible bits go first. Though we were coming to our fourth full season on the *Oceanic*, we still had plans for big recoveries, which pays quite a tribute to the quality and quantity of the fittings.

We gambled. If we could get up to Shetland mid- to latish-March, then we might just be able to take advantage of an early spell of decent weather and have an extra load away very quickly. Normally the weather didn't fit into a settled pattern until May, but we decided to take the chance.

We left Tayport on the 19th, as usual laden to the gunwales—mountains of food and supplies for ourselves and the islanders, fence posts, wires, agricultural implements and so on. In addition, the St Andrews Institute of Maritime Archaeology was planning a further season's excavation on the *Gran Grifon* site on Fair Isle, and technician Tony Long came along for the ride with their heavy plant.

It was a winter as opposed to a summer sea that we experienced. It looked heavy, grey and leaden, and generally inhospitable. *Trygg*, even with her bulky cargo, was kicking about violently, and it was an exhausted crew that drew abeam of Fair Isle the following evening, with darkness dropping fast and a heavy sea belting in from the north east.

Fair Isle has a nice sheltered little haven—how often we wished we could take it to Foula with us! Sheltered that is, except from the wind and seas from the north east. It was amazing that, time and again, a decision to go to see our friends on Fair Isle would immediately draw a blustery blow from the north. With our radar out of action—thank goodness we had had plenty of previous experience of navigating without radar—we had to come in to the tricky, swirling waters round the modest pier in almost total darkness.

While we crew members hung over the gunwales looking for skerries and rocks around the confused entrance, Alec wrestled hard with the wheel. It was either that or a night spent dodging in the lee of the cliffs, and none of us fancied that in the pitch black. The entrance to the haven had to be taken at speed, and one moment we were nearly on the rocks and the next almost on to the beach. As we tied up, and I moved ashore to telephone the news of our arrival, Tony shouted to me: 'Tell my wife I'm very brave!' He now realised that our tales of Shetland seas were not just exaggerated bar-talk.

A couple of days later we finished our journey with the short trip to Foula. We were pleased to find it calm at the pier, and while Alec and John Andrew saw to the unloading of all the cargo, I slipped into my wetsuit and swam out into the Voe to connect the up-and-down chain of our mooring and check all the shackles. Our moorings were ready for *Trygg*.

It was far from being reef-diving weather, but we had plenty to do. All our equipment—the stuff we had brought up, and the equipment already stored in the Haa for the winter—had to be taken out, cleaned and checked. Because it was so early in the year, each day we checked and rechecked our anchors, chains and shackles, renewing, as we always did, anything remotely worn.

A typical entry from the diary reads: 'Very windy from the north. Considerable swell. Driving snow. Boat kicking about but seems OK.' We were busy with preparations and praying for a moderation so we could really get cracking.

On the morning of 30 March, conditions in the Voe were reasonable, though the seas looked ominous outside. The wind was in the south west, and therefore both the boat and the Voe were in the lee. By afternoon the conditions were getting worse when the wind shifted to the south, and we had the chance of running for shelter to the Shetland mainland. But we would have had a very hazardous trip across and we judged, wrongly, that with the forecast of moderation and a swing to the south west we would be best to sit it out.

It was to be our last chance. Conditions got worse and worse, and soon we would really have been risking our necks even to travel out to *Trygg* in our inflatable, moored inside the pier and in considerable distress itself. Soon after that, we had no choice at all. Heavy crashing seas were breaking right across the Voe and the swell came tearing in as the gale increased. It would be impossible to take the boat out, and if we tried we would certainly be battered to death on the rocks. This somehow made it easier, for there was no decision to make and there was nothing we could do but wait, pray for moderation, and trust in our moorings.

It was Shetland's worst gale of the winter. We were confident of our moorings—thank goodness we had checked them so meticulously—but we were afraid if *Trygg* took much more of such a sea the shackle to the steel fitting on the deck would give way. Spray and spume, whipped up by the tearing gale, soaked everything far inshore. The wind howled and shrieked, so fierce that it was near impossible to stand up in. *Trygg*, the brave little survivor who had battled through a war and many a storm afterwards, fought for her very life as the mountainous seas threatened at any moment to engulf her. Would she roll right over? She had never, never let us down, but now that she was really in dire trouble she was on her own.

We all went to bed. It was distressing to watch her, and there was nothing we could do to improve the situation. Of course we didn't sleep a wink, and the wind seemed likely to tear the slates off the roof and burst through the windows. Above the noise we listened for the crash that would signal the end. . . . We listened avidly to the shipping forecasts—Scottish inshore waters, Radio 2, even the Norwegian one—praying for that hint of moderation. Soon after midnight Alec heard a faint 'chink chink'.

He shouted to me, and in seconds we made our way out. As we cowered against the gale, oilskins wrapped round us and eyes half-closed in the tearing wind, the smell told us she was finished even before we saw her. The reek of diesel. There was just enough light to see *Trygg* lying bow towards the pier on the rocks right in front of the Haa, with massive seas crashing right over her. She was as heavily built a 50-footer as I have ever seen, but as we watched, the most ghastly rending sound—almost like a shriek—came to us through the gale as the sturdy beams tore apart. 'We've had enough of this,' said Alec. 'Let's go inside.'

We were both numbed, appalled, stunned. Certainly in a place like Foula such a disaster was always on the cards, and many people had said we'd never manage to keep a boat that size in the Voe. Neither of us is particularly sentimental but, quite apart from the fact that *Trygg* was absolutely vital to our work, we both had a tremendous affection for her. It was almost as if she was a person, and I remember having that twisted, miserable feeling in my stomach as she disintegrated on the rocks. There was even a slight feeling of unreality, that this thing we had feared so often was actually happening.

No more than three minutes later we went out again, and there was nothing to be seen. Three minutes earlier it had been a boat, albeit doomed, that battered on the rocks. Now we could see nothing. Our troubles for the night were far from over, for we had a brand new inflatable and outboard engine moored inside the pier. Huge seas piled unceasingly over the pier, and we could get nowhere near the boat. Timbers, spars, beams and ropes were swept across the breakwater, narrowly missing our inflatable.

It was first light before we recovered it. The surging wreckage had quickly worn and snapped the mooring ropes on the inflatable, but amazingly it floated free and largely undamaged in the Voe. It was topped up with water, and the fuel tank, masks and other gear had gone, but the engine, though completely drenched, was still fixed to the transom stern.

Even by morning, when the storm and the sea had subsided considerably, water was still coming over in great lumps even as far up as the crane. Taking advantage of a brief lull when the inflatable came in near to the pier, Alec launched himself off and landed, half in the turbulent water, gripping the side of the boat.

Grabbing a floating spar, he paddled the boat to the rocks where, aided by some of the islanders—who were by this stage like us soaked to the skin—we managed to drag it ashore as successive breakers crashed over us. Two pontoons were badly torn in the recovery, but we had thought that we would lose the whole inflatable. We took it into the old, disused shop, where it was scrubbed down with fresh water, dried by paraffin heaters, and carefully stuck together again—a long painstaking job!

Meanwhile the whole Voe was just a mass of white, bubbling and foaming water, with planks, spars and sections of decking bobbing about all over the place. I remember wondering, while working on the *Adelaar* wreck in Barra, how more than 200 people could be drowned, with no survivors, when the ship struck so close to the shore. Surely the law of averages would ensure that by some freak at least one person would be cast ashore alive?

When I saw for myself exactly what happened to a wooden boat driven ashore in such a gale I understood why no Dutchman got off the *Adelaar*. Anyone on the *Trygg* could have jumped on to the rocks, only to be whisked off by the next wave, and battered to pieces in seconds. As we said at the time: 'If you are going to be shipwrecked, be on dry land when you do it!' Like the *Oceanic, Trygg* had not lasted long in a Shetland gale.

Winds of nearly 60 knots had been recorded at Sumburgh airport, which is a pretty strong blow, though they have experienced winds on Foula nearly three times as strong as that—fortunately when we weren't there! For us the blow came from the worst possible direction, and there was a very disturbed sea even before the wind whipped up. Once we were caught there, *Trygg* had no real chance of surviving. We did not yet know what part of the anchoring system had eventually failed, but we were surprised that our boat had lasted in those conditions for so long.

The next few days were spent generally tidying up. We managed to rescue many of our mooring and lifting ropes and mercifully, as it was the very start of the season, *Trygg* was about as empty as she ever was. All our main gear was being checked over in the Haa, where it was perfectly safe—though, mind you, islanders had told us that 'the gale of the century' had whipped up such a big sea in 1901 that the Haa fire was put out by the waters, and you will be able to imagine just how big a sea that must have been!

Everything was driven into the Voe rather than out to sea, though eventually a lot of timber drifted away and turned up all over Shetland. The next time we arrived on Fair Isle the first thing we saw on the beach was a part of *Trygg*—we even recognised which part! When *Trygg* broke up, her life raft somehow wasn't smashed to pieces like the rest of the boat, but inflated itself and drifted inside the pier that night—it was eventually torn apart when we tried to recover it in the same way as we had the inflatable.

We were concerned that a passing ship might spot floating wreckage and start off a search alert, so we quickly notified the Coastguard authorities on the Shetland mainland. The biggest single lump—part of the starboard side with our double sheathing—weighed a ton or so, and had been tossed far up the Ham Burn, so far that a casual visitor would wonder how it reached there. Many an hour I used to spend up the burn in battle with the wily brown trout, with my small stick—or wand as they call it up there—and worm-baited hook. When I first went to Foula I never dreamt that I would catch a brown, burn trout, under *Trygg's* starboard side, but it eventually happened!

After such high hopes of success, you can imagine we were temporarily in the depths of despair. But when we took stock of the situation, things didn't look quite so bleak. On the credit side, no one had been lost. *Trygg* had been totally wiped out, so we weren't faced with the problem of deciding—as we would have had to were she badly damaged—whether she was worth repairing or not. And, most important of all, she was well insured by the gentlemen of Lloyds.

'Look at it this way,' said Alec. 'Once you put aside the sentiment, we've just lost a tool. If we lose a hammer on the wreck when we are working, we come to the surface and get another one. We've lost a boat so we'll go out to get a replacement.'

Our insurance had been placed on the London market by Andy Beattie, who handles most of the marine insurance in Shetland. The rules normally dictate that when there is a coastal casualty, the insurance company sends a man to survey the wreck. However, Andy knew Foula well enough to realise that there wouldn't be much of a wreck to survey, and that it would be almost impossible to get into Foula in such bad weather anyway!

The underwriters accepted the situation, asking that we get 'an official' on Foula to state in writing that he saw the boat one night and the pile of wreckage the following morning. It would be hard to demonstrate to the firm, based in a warren in London where you can't move for officials, that Foula couldn't muster even *one* among its ranks (one of Foula's many wonderful attractions!), so it was eventually decided that Harry, as a subpostmaster, could very nearly qualify in the broader sense of the word. He signed a statement and all was well.

However, it should be stated that the underwriters treated us very well, and the claim was settled more quickly than I would ever have expected. They even accepted the gamble of our new boat versus the unpredictabilities of Ham Voe though, as you can imagine, they slapped on a pretty hefty premium.

We were very curious as to what had actually broken to cause the wrecking. The most likely answer, we reckoned, was that the up-and-down chain had torn loose where it was shackled to a heavy metal fitting on the deck. When the weather moderated sufficiently two days later we had the chance to find out.

Poor old *Trygg* was quite a sight! Virtually nothing remained of her hull, apart from a few timbers trapped under the engine. Her small propeller and shaft came out from in *front* of her engine, rather than aft. I'll never know how she got into such a position. The boat had been tossed so high on the rocks that the engine was virtually showing at low water. We could see where part of the rock itself had been broken off in the violent exchange between rock and boat. There was the winch, practically tied in a knot! We looked where the bow had been, and there was the chain still shackled into the metal fitting. Something else must have gone.

It was strange to dig about in the remains of a boat that had been so special to us, almost like rummaging about in a grave. But diving on her, we no longer had the same feeling for her. If you're being sentimental, what better way is there for a fine, little old ship to end her days than in a losing battle with the elements she had beaten so long? *Trygg's* great days were long behind her, and she would probably have ended up rotting and falling apart by some harbour wall. This way she went out on a top note.

I thought we were a bit over-sentimental about *Trygg* until I talked with a leading British salvage officer, Eric Stamford of United Towing, who has worked on salvage jobs all over the world. 'I've never lost that feeling of utter elation when we take a boat off the sands or the rocks,' he told me. 'It is not just that the operation is a success, but you realise that the ship will be sailing again. A ship to me is almost like a person. In the same way, it is a very sad moment for me each time we have to open the sea-cocks on a ship to scuttle her.'

When we inspected the other moorings we had another big surprise. Such had been the fury of the sea, that little *Trygg* had started to drag *Oceanic*'s mighty anchor! An anchor designed to hold 30,000 tons of ship had been dragged by our 50-footer—though only about 6 ft or so. The narrow confines of the Voe meant we hadn't been able to lay out as much chain as we would have liked, but nonetheless we would never have believed the 9-ton anchor would move, even in such a ferocious sea. A 7/8 in ground chain—only recently closely inspected—had broken and *Trygg* had dragged on to the two ½-ton anchors. Those too had quickly come free and *Trygg* was pushed on to the rocks.

We recovered some equipment that had remained on *Trygg*, such as the heavy lifting blocks and some shackles, but much of it had already been dispersed or buried. A large section of the keel, still carrying concrete ballast, was found some 60 yd away at the other side of the Voe. Goodness only knows how it got there!

The moorings had dragged right over to the north side of the Voe, and the chains were bar tight. It was a lengthy and complicated operation to dismantle them from *Trygg*'s remains, and using the lifting bag, to get them back to their correct position in the Voe. The *Oceanic*'s anchor could be left where it was, but the two schooner anchors had to be lifted again, and dropped in their correct position. We doubled up the chains, and dropped heavy cast-iron fittings from the *Oceanic* on top of them as added security. No boat would ever be safe in Ham Voe, but we were satisfied that our new mooring was as good as it would ever be.

We had had to search high and low for *Trygg* when we were looking for our first boat, but we were very much more fortunate with the replacement, *Valorous*. We first met Tommy Clark in

20 (*left*) The less glamorous side of salvage. With hammer and chisel, Alec batters at the white metal on one of the shoes from the thrust block. It is back-breaking work, and bruised hands and lost fingernails are the frequent result (*Alison McLeay*)

21 (*below*) a typical sight in *Valorous*'s spacious steel hold. Massive, twisted copper pipes lie among valves and other fittings. To the left, in bins, are some loose brass condenser tubes, broken in half, while in the foreground are the brass teeth from one of the anchor windlasses. In the background, held by a rope strop, is the 8 cwt steel beam which nearly killed Alec in our final full season.

22 The end of our work on the *Oceanic*. *Valorous*'s ground chain moorings are winched ashore at Tayport. The large links came from the *Oceanic*'s own anchor chain, and still have many years of life ahead of them (*Alison McLeay*)

1972, when he was a member of the rival team on the *Adelaar* wreck on Barra. He was a quiet, reserved lad, just getting on with his job, and there was certainly no 'aggro' between us. The bosses were fighting it out in the courtrooms, but there was no real tension between the workers as we waited our turn for diving on the reef. If they had got into trouble, which they might have done on one slightly wild day, we would have motored in to help them, and I'm sure they would have helped us in the same circumstances. Off site we kept ourselves generally to ourselves, but had the occasional beer together.

We ran into Tommy again in Shetland. He had come up to work on pier-construction sites and oil-related work as a diver, but liked the place and stayed. He bought a boat that had originally been the Skerries-registered *St Clair*, but had been converted into a boat that would carry fish offal from Lerwick to the 'gut factory' in the nearby island of Bressay. She had a solid, heavy steel hold fitted in her, a superior Norwegian hydraulic winch, and a long derrick so that she could work whatever the height of the tide. By necessity, she had a Board of Trade loadline.

We met Tommy a few times up there; he had bought *Valorous* when she had outlived her usefulness at the 'gut factory'. He did the occasional contract job with her, ran some small cargoes around Shetland, and occasionally took her to a wreck. However, a big contract came up on the Scottish mainland, and he laid *Valorous* up for the summer and sailed off by the steamer from Lerwick.

When he heard of the *Trygg* disaster, he made an extremely generous offer. 'I'll not be using her this summer,' he told us by telephone. 'Just take her away and use her,' he added, as casually as if he was lending us a couple of quid for a drink.

We could hardly get over the generosity of his offer, but pointed out that we had lost one boat at Foula, and there was no real guarantee that we wouldn't lose another!

So we agreed to buy the boat from him, pay him the cash, and offer it back to him at the end of the summer—he was not entirely sure what his plans would be. As things turned out his south contract continued and he decided not to take up his option of re-purchase. That suited us just fine, and *Valorous* was quickly to show up many of *Trygg*'s shortcomings.

We sailed for Foula on 21 May with our fine new boat and by 5 June were travelling south with our first full load. Tommy had said he would hold our cheque for a week or two, and during that interval the insurers paid up on *Trygg*'s loss. By coincidence our cheque was presented to the bank on the same day as we banked our first scrap cheque, so we didn't even have to borrow heavily to buy the *Valorous*.

Valorous is 62 ft, 12 ft longer than *Trygg*, and of course there was that much less room in the narrow Voe. We put wires round bulky rock structures on the north and south sides of the Voe, so in the event of poor weather a heavy rope could be laid from *Valorous*'s bow to the shore. This meant less weight was put on the actual mooring chains, though of course we had to look sharpish if the wind swung right round, as the rope could then foul under the boat. This operation took about half an hour to prepare, but when it came to sound sleeping in dubious conditions, the knowledge that the extra rope was out was far better than any sleeping pill!

It was a joy to work scrap on a boat with such a winch and with such a hold. One problem we used to have on *Trygg* was with the length of the strops. Sometimes a diver would strop a load, and the strop would be just too long. When the lifting hook came to the top of the derrick—and the lift could not be continued—we would sometimes find that the brass was still lower than the gunwale. At best there was a long struggle of tying off and blocking, and at worst the lump had to be lowered again. With *Valorous*'s sophisticated and well-designed gear, we had plenty of height for lifting.

Trygg's relatively small hold entrance meant we often had great piles on the deck, which had to be cut up before stowing, in any case a cramped and difficult operation. When the hatch-boards were taken from the *Valorous* the entire hold was revealed and moreover, with the steel lining, heavy lumps of brass could be swung over the gunwale and dropped straight away—thus eliminating the pendulum effect which can be so dangerous.

Valorous was not equipped with bow lifting gear like the *Trygg*, but fortunately almost all the big lumps were removed from the Shaalds before *Trygg's* wrecking. Much of the final condenser remained on the reef, and we decided it would be simpler to try to lift it in pieces out there than to reconstruct another bowlift, bring the piles of tubes into the Voe, and work on it there.

Imagine 9 tons of tubes, lying in a pile on the bottom; the diver has to strop about 2 tons of them at a time. The only way to do this was to put a strop round about quarter of the pile at the end of the tubes, and uptide of the *Valorous*. The diver would take a special signal rope down with him, and give the heave-up signal.

The tubes would start to rise, and when they were tipped up maybe a foot or two, the diver had to signal for the lift to stop. Then another strop was passed round the middle of the tubes and they were dropped again. In theory, when they were bundled round the middle they could be lifted aboard in a coherent manner.

We had a few problems. If the strop slipped off-centre the tubes could take a vertical rather than horizontal position, and many of the tubes would slip out like arrows raining on top of the diver—the most frustrating thing to happen, as the diver couldn't do anything about it! Sometimes it was hard for the diver to slip the strop round the bundle, and I remember once having difficulty in completing the operation. I needed another pair of hands, and the only way I could see of achieving the right result was to swim *under* the precariously stropped tubes. Looking back on it, I took a stupid risk but I was tired, frustrated and pig-sick of condenser tubes, and I had to continue with the job till it was done. I had a good look at the first strop, decided it would hold, and swam through very quickly indeed!

Alec and I both took similar risks at times, I think particularly when we were tired and frustrated. We had to complete the work, and we were working for ourselves. If we were working for a nationalised industry, or even a private contractor, we would have come up and said: 'No, we can't manage that task safely.' It is a fine attitude if you are getting your wages anyway! We only managed forty or so days each year on the Shaalds and we had to make them pay. If we didn't bring up brass we didn't eat.

Another great advantage of our new hold was that a bundle of tubes would fit straight into it, without needing to be broken up. We telephoned our metal merchant in Glasgow, and he agreed to take tubes, end plates and centre plates still all fixed together. The biggest grind in scrap breaking was removed from us.

We still weren't satisfied with one part of our lifting rig—the gooseneck where the derrick and mast meet. '*Trygg*'s was a much better design,' we recalled, and then realised that *Trygg* could still provide the solution. A quick search of the Voe found *Trygg*'s gooseneck, still attached to what was now a twisted lump of metal. This was dragged out over the rocks, the gooseneck was cut out, and we headed for Scalloway where our old deckhand, Andrew Ratter, a qualified man at Moore's yard, welded it up together into the *Valorous* rig. We felt much safer after that.

You can never be too careful with lifting gear, because if it breaks you can have a most fearful accident with a derrick crashing on to the deck. We once broke a chain—which fortunately had a back-up rope which held, although it should have broken before the chain. It so worried us that we renewed all the riggings on the derrick and mast.

Within a month of getting *Valorous*, and aided by a glorious spell of weather, we had two loads lifted and away. *Trygg* was a fine little boat, but perhaps her papers would not have satisfied a strict Board of Trade man or customs officer, so we always tended to use our own quiet little port, where we were known. With *Valorous*, with all her official niceties in order, we could sail into any port with our heads held high.

So we decided to use Scrabster, just off the notorious Pentland Firth, on the north Scottish mainland. It was a twelve hour trip, and we were made very welcome by the harbourmaster, officials and fishermen. Scrabster had much better unloading facilities than Tayport, which is only rarely used for cargo nowadays, and we managed a quick turnround back to Foula. For the shorter journey Alec and John Andrew could easily manage the boat by themselves, while I rode shotgun on the scrap lorry on the way to the yard in Glasgow! I then flew back up to join the team. The whole operation took only a few days.

It was very appropriate that we should land in Scrabster, for the *Oceanic* had lain in nearby Thurso Bay and Scapa Flow shortly before she was wrecked. Several folk remembered her, and some of the other great ships of that era, and when the local paper up there ran a short story about our arrival in the port, correspondence was carried out at length for weeks afterwards by folk who remembered about the *Oceanic* and others. It was the first time I realised what feelings of magnificence and splendour are still conjured up by memories of the massive great steamships of the early twentieth century.

It can be a wild spot, and the famous tides of the Firth can make the Shaalds look like a trickle. A lot of shipping passes through the narrow gap, and we were as near as dammit hit on one occasion by a large tanker which came tearing through on a misty day. We didn't see him on the radar till rather late, as we were trying to verify our position in relation to Orkney and the Scottish mainland. There was some hopping about on *Valorous* for a moment or two, I can assure you!

With the scuttled Scapa fleet, or the remains of it, so close by, the older fishermen are full of the tales of salvage. Many was the wrecking yarn we heard—my other happy memory is of steaks that used to cover the whole of a large ashet at the Scrabster Hotel, particularly welcome to men who had been living out of tins for too long!

Valorous was also highly suited to the job of taking the *Oceanic* propeller blades out from Foula to the Shetland mainland. We decided it would be unpractical to take them all south with us, when they could easily be shipped, either to English markets or to the Continent. There is always a considerable danger that scrap will be stolen, but even the most determined casual thief would find it hard to walk off with 6 tons all in one lump. The blades were protected by their size.

With *Trygg* we had managed to get all eleven blades safely under the mail-boat crane and lifted clear into nearby Ladycap Geo. Two had already been taken away, which meant there were nine others to be transferred. It was a job that could only be carried out when *Valorous* was empty and at the high spring tides.

We calculated that we would have to take *Valorous* right inside the pier until her bow was on the rocks. There would only be a few inches under the keel (which is why the hold had to be empty to start with). and obviously once the blade or blades went in, the boat would sink deeper into the water. If too much weight was put into the hold, then the keel would go fast on the bottom.

Simple, you might say. Just lift the blades out again and the boat will rise once more. But the problem was that the crane could only reach just forward of the hold, and each blade had to be manually pushed towards the stern as it was lowered—making it very difficult to get them out again. When the tide ebbed and the water drained out, the loaded boat would be left high and dry on a hard bottom, which would do it no good at all.

The first day we tried, the tide barely rose high enough, but we did manage to load one. This was run to Scalloway, where it was lifted by crane. We were back for the next high water, when another was loaded; then there were two batches of two, and on the biggest tide of the cycle, we just managed the remaining three. There was some excitement on this load, for the boat stuck fast after the third blade. However, the crane was attached to the *Valorous* winch barrels. When the crane was pulled up a foot or so the bow lifted and *Valorous*, with several islanders heaving at a rope to the stern like a tug-of-war team, slid off into deeper water. We now had all the blades, apart from Mrs Blewett's one off Ireland!

It was also anxious work loading them, for the Foula crane sometimes lowered its loads slightly 'out of control'. The braking system wasn't quite 100 per cent, and while this didn't really matter in lowering the mail boat into the water, 6 tons of metal dropped from a height unhindered, would be quite liable to go through the bottom of the boat!

At Scalloway all ten blades were loaded on to three lorries and transported through to the Hay & Co yard in Lerwick—from where they could easily be loaded on ship for their final destination. Of the heavy lifts, only the bosses now remained.

Valorous was lying happily at her moorings, but we could never relax with her. Every time we walked out of the house we thought: 'Will she be sitting happily at the mooring, or has something gone wrong?' Even on relatively fine nights we would each wake up perhaps two or three times, and not go to sleep again until we had checked on her safety. We had always feared that we would lose a boat, but had suspected that *Trygg* would be all right. One loss was understandable—two would be unbearable.

Despite the disastrous start we had by far our most successful season, recovering some 60 tons, and moving all the propeller blades into the bargain. We also had the opportunity of looking at the wreck of a small German trawler, the *Castor*, lost just before World War I on the island of Burra (close to the Shetland mainland). It was on a relatively easy site, though slightly deeper than the *Oceanic*—perhaps 80 ft at its deepest. It was a break for us all, and we made a few recoveries. John Andrew told us when he surfaced: 'I really enjoyed the dive, but I kept feeling that something was wrong, or missing. Then I realised the difference was I wasn't battling against a tide.' We explained that all wrecks weren't in as bad spots as the *Oceanic*!

As the season dragged to a close, we again held on, trying to get that little bit of extra scrap. It was to no avail, and once

September arrived Alec and Moya spent two weeks on end sheltering in Scalloway. Eventually we decided that we would get no more from the Shaalds and just wanted to get *Valorous* back to Foula for the day so that we could load up with some loose brass from our yard—all the bits and pieces we had stored over the years—and take some of our equipment south.

We started our best-ever season with shipwreck, and we were not so far from finishing it the same way. Again, moderate conditions turned to very nasty conditions frighteningly quickly.

On the morning we left the weather was fine enough for us to consider going out to the reef to dive and cut off all our wreck moorings (the winter gales would take them if we didn't), but we decided it would be a bit risky. We had agreed to take fourteen of Foula's famous 'moorit' or coloured sheep to Fair Isle where Barry Sinclair, the shopkeeper and a good friend for many years, wanted to start breeding the 'Foula sheep' for the colour of their fleeces. Fair Isle was almost on our route south, so we said we would be happy to drop them off for him.

The swell became worse and worse all through the morning, and from the start it would have been impossible for us to come into the pier. The wind wasn't that bad, but a long and heavy swell was throwing *Valorous* all over the place. Alec stayed on the boat with the engine running, so that he could do something if the moorings broke or dragged. We loaded all our equipment with the inflatable. Now for the sheep!

We looked anything but salvage men as we loaded half the sheep, legs tied together to keep them quiet. Several islanders were down at the pier to help, and Jim Gear and Andrew Ratter were in the inflatable helping me. I think all of us, including the sheep, found the first trip out to a very lively *Valorous* a lumpy affair.

We were just coming alongside the pier, ready to tie up to collect the remaining seven sheep, when I suddenly spotted a huge wave coming straight for us. 'The pier will take most of that,' I thought—and then, crash! This solid lump of water smashed into us, though fortunately we all managed to hang on.

We were soaked from head to foot, and the inflatable was completely brimming with water.

They were having their adventures on the pier too. A tractor and trailer was in the process of delivering the sheep, but the islanders on the pier saw the wave coming and rushed up the hill to safety. The sheep were not so fortunate, and the single rogue wave broke over pier, tractor and trailer, submerging the sheep. Mercifully it didn't take the tractor and trailer off the pier into the water, the the luckless sheep started floating over the built-up sides of the trailer. Just in time, the islanders rushed back to grab the unfortunate beasts, and we were very lucky not to lose any. The inflatable was sorted out quickly, and the remaining sheep delivered to *Valorous*, wet, miserable, and bewildered.

By this time Alec was jumping up and down on deck, screaming at us to hurry up. The big wave had swung *Valorous* out to a crazy angle, and the sooner we were out of the Voe the better. Such was the excitement that the schoolchildren were allowed out specially to see the departure, and we nearly gave them an extra spectacular show.

We tied a rope to our up-and-down chain, slackened the chain off, and cut the rope loose. That way we were able to steam right ahead with no danger of fouling. The sheep were gathered on the deck in makeshift pens, and I moved about to ensure they didn't fall and get trampled. There was a heavy swell when we left the isle, but there was no danger to us in open sea. As we nosed past Foula's war memorial, down towards the south end of the isle, and then set course for Fair Isle, I remembered what Alfie Jamieson, of the *Alis Wood*, told me what he thought about Foula, Ham Voe and the pier, with regard to his boat's safety.

'Foula is a grand place,' he said with a wry smile. 'It's a grand place to get to hell out of!'

In those conditions, he certainly was right!

8

Success and Near-disaster

Our final season on the *Oceanic* was to be 1978, and we had two main objectives. The supply of scrap was dwindling, but we wanted to make a thorough job of cleaning up, and, secondly, we had to get the two propeller bosses to Scalloway, an operation we felt sure would cause us a lot of problems.

With any luck, as we didn't have a large workload planned, we would at last have the chance of visiting other wreck sites round Shetland.

This time we made our way up from Tayport much later in the year—early May, in fact—having learned from bitter experience that arriving earlier was a waste of time and a worthless risk. We also brought up John Andrew's newly purchased boat on the deck of the *Valorous*, firmly lashed and posing few problems, apart from the fact that we couldn't see very well out of the wheelhouse!

The season started well enough, and there was soon some 12 tons of assorted scrap in the hold of the boat. All seemed to be on course for a glorious final summer, when out of the blue we were suddenly hit by something we had dreaded from the beginning, but somehow never thought would happen—a serious accident.

As I said earlier, contrary to popular belief, we had always felt we were more likely to have problems working in the hold with heavy pieces of scrap, or on deck at the receiving end of a snapped strop-wire, than actually diving on the *Oceanic*. This particular day we had decided that it wasn't quite good enough weather to go out to the Shaalds, and Alec, John Andrew and I went out in the inflatable to *Valorous*'s moorings to shift some of the scrap in the hold so that the boat would be correctly trimmed.

Like many accidents, this one should never have happened. A steel beam weighing about 8 cwt lay fore and aft on top of the hold—it was designed to hold the hatchboards when they were put into place. The beam rested in metal slots, and could be lifted out of position from the top if the full width of the open hold was required for loading. We had left it in place while we were working below, and were saving ourselves all of 30 seconds by trying to drag a bearing across the hold rather than repositioning the derrick to lift it. It was a task we had carried out many times before.

Alec was directing operations from the bottom of the hold. Suddenly, the eye of the winch wire caught the long transverse beam, lifted one end slightly out of its slot, and allowed it to career down the wire—straight towards Alec.

If the falling beam had hit his head, that would have been the end of Alec, but mercifully he spotted it a fraction of a second before it reached him. As he tried to leap out of the way, his back came up hard against a solid lump of brass casing. The falling beam, hissing down the winch wire, caught him full in the guts, crushing him painfully in a monstrous vice of brass and steel.

Alec has always been a lad with an outsize appetite, and we often used to tease him about it, insisting that he must have cast-iron innards. Perhaps there's some truth in the rumour—who knows—since it had seemed inevitable that he would have been cut in half. I was sure his entire rib-cage would have been smashed, though it transpired that he took the main blow on the left side just below the ribs.

Somehow, John Andrew and I got him out of the hold, across the deck of the *Valorous*, and over the side into the inflatable. Not one word was exchanged, as we realised we had to get Alec ashore as soon as possible. Within a couple of minutes we were at the pier, where Alec immediately collapsed in agony.

He obviously needed hospital attention immediately. Maggie was on her rounds at the south end of the island, and the nurse's car was out of action. She was quickly collected, however, and after a brief examination established that Alec's condition wasn't dangerous, although he certainly ought to be sent to hospital at once.

There we were on an island 25 miles from the mainland, in as remote a spot as you can find in Britain. Yet the ironic fact is that Alec was probably in hospital faster than if he had had a similar accident on his farm in Fife. Loganair's Islander air-craft—which has saved many lives since the company started flying in Shetland in the late 1960s—arrived with a doctor from Sumburgh and in no time the patient was safely delivered to the Gilbert Bain Hospital in Lerwick. The National Health Service takes plenty of brickbats, but not from us.

Looking back at the incident long after Alec had recovered, there was one part of it all which really amused us. We had all been handling cast iron from the bottom of the sea, and such metal gives off a near-indelible black dye. In addition, all of us—especially Alec—were in our roughest, filthiest clothes, rather like Black and White Minstrels fallen upon hard times.

When he arrived at the hospital, in a bad way, he was immediately stripped—Moya said his clothes weren't long in coming out of the back door. A young student nurse was instructed to clean a small patch on the arm of this black apparition with the Al Jolson eyes, so that a saline drip could immediately be set up. The poor girl couldn't even get a little bit of him clean.

All soaps, solvents and grease removers failed. They eventually got their small clean patch with hard scrubbing, using floor polish! I bet that treatment doesn't feature in the instruction manuals!

Alec was massively bruised all over, and had crushed one kidney and damaged it badly. We were glad he was alive, but it did seem our salvage activities would be over for the year when he signed the documents for removal of part of the kidney. He won a reprieve, however, when the doctors decided that because he was young and very fit, the internally damaged kidney might heal up on its own.

He had many days of intense pain, but was released after a fortnight, confident he would soon be back directing operations and doing light work. He looked pale and drawn when he returned, and the doctors' estimate of a six-week lay-off proved very accurate.

John Andrew and I ran the *Valorous* to Scalloway, since we decided that if we couldn't lift with her she would be safer there. With *Valorous* in the Voe we needed two fit men at the Haa ready to leave at a moment's notice, in case anything happened to her, and I would be unable to take the boat out by myself. Meanwhile John Andrew and I continued work on the *Oceanic* from the inflatable.

Alec made a marvellous recovery, and long before he was fit to dive again he was on the deck of *Valorous* directing operations. The summer wasn't a write-off after all, and soon after he recovered we shipped a load south to Scrabster.

We now turned our attention to the bosses. With a mixture of lifting bags and small explosive charges we removed the pinned steel keys and the section of propeller shaft from the bosses, though the operation didn't go completely smoothly—one expensive 5 ton bag had a hole blown in it, and many hours were spent stitching and glueing in carrying out the repair.

We had assumed that two 5 ton lifting bags would raise each boss, and planned, if we could lift them high enough under the bags, to pull them in to the point of the pier. To our surprise, even with a 10 ton lift attached, the first boss stayed firmly on the bottom; our only option was to rig up a simple block-and-tackle system, to assist the lifting bags.

It was a tricky, complicated operation, and everything had to be just right. We were further held up when Alec's health broke down again during preparations for the lift. Both of us had been diving on the bosses, despite the fact that Alec had been troubled with headaches for some days—this meant popping up and down repeatedly, a bad thing if you have any pressure problems lurking in such areas as sinuses. By lunchtime one day Alec had a blinding headache, and went off to bed. The headache turned into regular bouts of sickness, failing vision and lack of strength in his grip. With fog threatening to come in, Maggie decided to call in the ambulance plane once more, in case Alec's condition worsened and he couldn't leave the island.

After his previous problems we were very concerned about his fitness. For the second time that summer, Foula's rickety old stretcher was put together and Alec was carted off to the airstrip. The hospital examined him once more and diagnosed a small pocket of high-pressure air in his sinuses, rather more serious than mere sinus inflammation. He was soon discharged, but his diving for the summer was over.

We thought carefully about the bosses during our second enforced break, and came to the conclusion that there was no way we could lift them high enough to pull them into the shallow water at the end of the pier. The only other answer was to sling them, one at a time, under the bow of the *Valorous* and—this was the tricky bit—take them, dangling under the boat, over 25 miles of open sea to Scalloway.

Wooden beams—old bits of poor *Trygg*—were laid out on the deck forward, and heavy wires slung round and round the boat. The beams meant that the load would be spread across the whole deck and not restricted to the gunwales, which wouldn't have stood such weight. I was to attach the two 5 ton bags to the boss, fill them so that 10 tons of lift were on, and stand by as boss and bags were lifted towards the surface by block and tackle. The boss would then be connected to the wires slung under the boat, and the bags slowly deflated until the full weight was taken up by *Valorous*'s bow.

After the crossing from Foula, we would run each boss into Scalloway at high water, and take it into the shallow water alongside the pier until it grounded on the sandy bottom. When the tide ebbed, the wires would slacken off and I could undo the shackles holding the boss. It was a long journey to transport each 12 ton weight, and with the boss dangling some 20 ft below the surface, it was to be awkward making our way through some of the shallows as we approached Scalloway.

John Andrew summed up the enterprise accurately when he said, 'A fine thing—off you go with the company profits for the year dangling on the end of a bit of string!' As a safety measure we towed the inflatable behind us all the way, ready to jump into it at the first sign of the *Valorous* turning over. As it turned out, though, both trips went like clockwork, and it's perhaps interesting to note that in all our salvage operations relating to the bosses we never lifted either of them more than 10 ft from the bottom. A crane was hired again at Scalloway, and it was an exciting moment for us and many others when the bosses saw the light of day for the first time since the *Oceanic* was wrecked. Soon they too were sent off by lorry to Hay & Co's yard.

And that was virtually the end of the season, and the whole *Oceanic* project. I dived a few more tides and scrounged some pipe forward, and cleaned up round the engines. Despite Alec's two accidents we had achieved our aims of retrieving the bosses and a fair load of scrap. The end came suddenly, when I surfaced after a dive to announce that the site was virtually clear. I cut off all the buoys, gave the propeller shaft a 'Good-bye and thanks' pat, and that was it.

It was mid-August, and still a fine spell, so we spent a couple of days tied up to the pier while we loaded the mountain of gear we had built up on Foula and cleaned out the Haa.

It was a sad moment, saying goodbye on the pier to the islanders who had been our friends for so many years. We weren't really sad to say farewell to the *Oceanic*—the upsets of the final year had knocked some of the stuffing out of us, and we were ready for the change. We'll be back to Foula and the *Oceanic* again for a short visit, but the real work has been done. It was a success beyond our wildest dreams.

Many great salvage feats have been performed over the years, and no doubt many more will be achieved in the future. Our operation was too small to be considered among the 'greats', and in any case we would never dream of putting the *Oceanic* on such a list. But we did create our records. Taking a very limited field—an exposed, broken-up and abandoned open-water shipwreck, and concentrating on the vessel's non-ferrous fittings rather than any cargo—then I've heard it said that we recovered more from the *Oceanic* than has been retrieved from any other steamship wreck. By 'more' I refer to quantity rather than value.

The propeller brass hasn't been weighed since we brought it up, but it seems likely that our combined weight of non-ferrous recoveries from the *Oceanic* will be nearer to 250 than 200 tons. Obviously this will realise a considerable sum of money, but not a vast figure when you take our costs and the length of time we committed to the wreck into account. A North Sea diver would dismiss as a pittance our salaries compared with his own, but I'll wager we've had a hundred times more satisfaction. We're particularly proud to have made these recoveries from an 'undiveable' wreck—and one to which no one else has been.

I won't claim that every single saleable piece of non-ferrous scrap has been removed from the site, but we recovered far more than we ever imagined we would. There were some risks which in our opinion no amount of scrap would justify, like wriggling into corners of the double bottom in pursuit of a piece of copper piping which had been swept into it, but there's nothing left now which would justify the attention of a commercially minded salvage man.

Alec is keener on salvage than ever, and recently formed Kilburns Salvage Co, based in Fife, which has taken over much of the Crawford & Martin plant. Now completely recovered from the health problems he had in the summer, he's continually planning new schemes and techniques for salvage. As I write this, early in 1979, his wife Moya runs their small farm, and Alec is out in *Valorous* in the Tay Estuary, helping to drag a small coaster off the beach where she has stuck.

John Andrew has carefully stored his diving suit and equipment, and is busy making creels and planning a major assault on the Foula lobster population along with Sam Davies. John Andrew's salvage efforts paid for his new boat and the opportunity to stay on the island he loves; he deserved every penny he made. We hope to see him when we travel to Shetland this summer, and perhaps we'll all have a nostalgic dive together.

I have less to do now with full-time salvage commitment, but hope and plan to dive with Alec from time to time. I suppose for me there will never be another *Oceanic*, and I want to come out at the top. I love diving, and look forward to the freedom of doing so just for enjoyment rather than with the obligation to achieve something each time I go into the water.

Will there ever be 'another *Titanic*' — or even 'another *Oceanic*' for that matter? I doubt it, but you don't say 'never' in the salvage business. Poor old Robbie Robertson was born fifty years too early, and you could say that we went into business five years too late (metal prices had largely slumped by the time we came on the scene). But money was never the whole story for us, and I for one would have gone through it all for a basic wage and the satisfaction of being one of three men who, in five years, had taken the heart from a monster ship which it had needed 1,500 workers to build in the Harland & Wolff yard. A glance through our financial accounts shows that the gross value of our recoveries has topped six figures.

Whether anyone in future will be able to do what we did is debatable. Equipment is now cripplingly expensive, making a small-scale operation like ours extremely difficult, and altering the economics of the kind of salvage work we carried out on the *Oceanic*. In addition, new proposed government legislation, designed to protect divers working on anything to do with oil, seems about to make independent professional diving almost impossible unless it is on a major scale. It would certainly have ruled out our operations on the *Oceanic*. This isn't the time or place to go into the details, but sometimes we feel it's rather like insisting that a climber has a rescue helicopter hovering overhead every time he sets foot on a mountain!

No—one way or another, it doesn't look as if there'll ever be another *Oceanic*!

Postscript

Alec's accident prevented us from finishing off our 1978 season as we would have liked—some main bearings and eccentrics on the *Oceanic*'s engines still lay on the Shaalds, and with the price of their white metal linings topping the £5,000-a-ton mark we felt we had to go back once more, albeit briefly.

At the same time we had our eye on another potentially rich wreck (that's *another* tale!), near our home base, but we felt a month spent on Foula early in the summer would produce worthwhile returns. Accordingly *Valorous* nosed out of Tayport early in May 1979 on the familiar run north.

On board with us this time was Bill White, a Fife man who had some experience of diving though not of wreck work. With John Andrew now working hard on his lobster boat *Lively* we needed a third hand for work on the reef. Our greatest concern was putting *Valorous* at risk again in Foula's often inhospitable Ham Voe, especially for only a month's salvage recoveries. But 'nothing ventured, nothing gained' was our final decision.

Perhaps because our visit was only to be a brief one, the Shetland Islands promptly gave us a command performance of their entire repertoire of 'summer' weather. Although it was mid-May we woke up one morning to find the hills covered in snow, and to the east the Shetland mainland just a slender ribbon of white on a grey sea. This was followed by two unpleasant south-easterly gales which brought the seas piling into the Voe, and sent *Valorous* scuttling for safety to the mainland. If we had forgotten, this only served to underline the unpredictability of the weather in the north.

We took advantage of a lull in the gales to locate the wreck again and fix the mooring buoys to the engine area where we would be working. This trip was so familiar to us by now that Alec not only succeeded in dropping me right on top of the wreck at the first attempt, but even managed to do it on the correct section of propeller shaft!

But the tides on the Shaalds lived up to their reputation for totally ignoring the printed tables, and the scheduled 'slack' time which we expected turned out to be a rushing southerly stream. In seconds the fast flowing flood had jammed me like a cork in a bottle hard between the propeller shaft and the wreckage underneath. As I turned my head to extricate myself the tide caught my mask and effortlessly tore it from my face. 'Yes, we're back on the Shaalds all right', I remember thinking—and at the same time feeling there must be an easier way of earning a crust.

When I had secured my mooring I quickly raced for the surface to signal the inflatable to come and pick it up. The boat was with me in moments, but by then the tide had me in its grip, and I was being pulled under the water. A ludicrous tug-o'-war ensued, with the end of the mooring line in my right hand and Alec and Bill trying to haul me in by my left. Eventually we got ourselves sorted out and reassured Bill—who was beginning to suspect that our worst tidal tales were under-stated—that things weren't always like that.

Our former island home of the Haa had severe roof damage from a hurricane the previous winter and was undergoing major repairs. Fortunately we were able to stay in the old shop from which the islanders witnessed the wrecking so many years before and which has recently been converted into a home by newly settled islander, Sam Davies.

When the weather moderated we managed to get on with the work in hand and the first thing to strike us—in contrast to the start of previous seasons—was how little loose brass was lying around, turned up by the winter seas. '*Somebody*'s had a good bit from this wreck,' we jested to Bill after his first dip.

Our plan was a simple one. Alec would concentrate on trying to free the remaining bearings from the heart of the engines, while Bill and I would take it in turns to fish around for any loose pieces of copper and brass we could find. For a change we would also gather as much lead scrap as possible—metal which in the days of plenty we scarcely bothered about, but which had recently risen so sharply on world markets that, pound for pound, it was more valuable than our propeller brass.

Soon we had lifted 30 cwt of the immensely valuable white metal and were clearing up the final lifts. We had another ton or so of copper and brass and about the same of lead. As the buoys were cut off for the final time we were still thinking of a big end half-shell bearing which we *might* have got, but a halt had to be called somewhere! As we left the reef for what will almost certainly be the last time, we felt a mixture of emotions. It is unlikely that we will ever be faced with a more dangerous wreck site, but those seven years had left us with a sound bank balance, a tremendous sense of achievement and profound gratitude for both being still in one piece.

Within a week of lifting our heavy moorings from the Voe and making the long trip south we were doing battle with the problems of lifting eight-ton slabs of six-inch armour plate from the wreck of the armoured cruiser *Argyll*. There will always be another wreck.

I have written earlier that there will never be another *Oceanic*, but the seas round Foula nearly claimed another monster prize just before we went north for the final time. A west-side fishing boat was amazed to spot a 100,000-ton oil tanker idly nosing through the shallows between Foula and Shetland—miles from his plotted course to the west and escaping wreck only by the greatest good fortune. A tanker loss would be a total disaster for the magnificent and unique bird and marine life round Shetland shores. And it wouldn't even be a real bonus to the salvage men. They don't build ships now as they did at Harland & Wolff at the turn of the century.

Appendix

Salvage Report

Alec Crawford

The physical salvage work on the *Oceanic* was made more complicated by the continual need for speed because of the strong tide and the exposed position of the wreck site. This allowed us only 192 days diving—a 'day' sometimes only being 20 minutes—to recover just under 250 tons of non-ferrous metal during the summer seasons of five and a half years. The maximum number of diving days we had during one season was forty-one, and the minimum twenty-nine.

As a result each particular salvage operation had to be meticulously planned, the part of the ship identified, its original method of construction researched, and the position and size of the explosive charges previously calculated, in order that as much as possible could be laid during each slack tide. The type and make of the *Oceanic*'s engines and auxiliary equipment were first observed when tidying up all the loose scrap in the engine-room area. Engineering reference books of that era were then consulted.

The steam-engine is an extremely simple machine relying on the expansion of water and water vapour as it is heated in the boiler, and the resultant pressurised steam acting on the faces of pistons to drive them up and down the cylinders in which they work. In the case of the *Oceanic*'s two engines, which were of the triple expansion type with four cylinders—there being two intermediate pressure cylinders—the steam first entered the high-pressure cylinder (the smallest cylinder), and then passed into the other cylinders in turn, expanding in each cylinder as it did the work. Each cylinder had to be larger than the last to accommodate the larger volume of steam at a lower pressure. Finally the steam was sucked from the low-pressure cylinder by the air pump into the condenser. The sea water circulating through the brass tubes in the condenser cooled the steam passing over the tubes, causing it to condense and fall to the bottom where it was pumped out and returned to the boilers as water. The up-and-down motion of the pistons was converted into a turning motion via connecting rods and the crank of the crankshaft, which in turn drove the propeller shafting. This very simply illustrates the principle and some of the machinery involved.

Of the 192 days we dived on the *Oceanic*, over half of these involved the use of the inflatable boat on its own—the inflatable was a more convenient and safer base when working with explosives, and could lie above the wreck more securely than the larger lifting vessel in marginal weather conditions. During conditions when it was impossible to lift, a diver could be clearing an area of pieces of brass and placing them in bins, while another diver laid explosive charges.

The 29 ton propellers were the largest single items of brass we concentrated on after the initial clean-up of loose non-ferrous metal. As they were both partly buried in wreckage, rock and concretion, seven tides were spent tunnelling beneath the starboard propeller and only three tides on the less-buried port propeller. A charge of 100 lb was used under both, placed so as to break two of the blades off (and the nut and the spinner), cut the shaft on the ship side of the propeller, and lift the boss clear of the wreckage. This was achieved satisfactorily on the port side but on the starboard side one blade remained and the boss lay in a hole in the wreckage. An extra 14 lb was then used to knock the remaining blade off, and roll the boss out of the hole and on to clear ground, ready for lifting. This charge was excessive, and a smaller one of 5 lb would have been quite sufficient. The propeller boss was webbed (partly hollow) and this allowed the charge to be placed underneath the base of the remaining blade.

The steering engines which lay alongside the propellers were stripped of most of their non-ferrous fittings including the large brass gearwheels which ran on to the rudder quadrant. Some of the smaller bearings were considered uneconomic to recover.

The tailshaft liners and sterntubes proved difficult and more expensive to extract than originally calculated. The tailshaft liners consisted of a gunmetal bush 1 in thick for the length of the sterntube and then 7/8th in thick up to the inner gland. The brass liner extended the full length of the shaft to prevent galvanic action taking place between the brass liner and the steel of the shaft. The sterntube was approximately 8 ft 6 in long and 1-5/16th in thick at the thickest part, which supported the lignum vitae bearing, and was only 11/16th in thick beneath the wood. John Penn invented the lignum vitae bearing in 1855. An outer gunmetal bush (sterntube) with an internal diameter slightly larger than the shaft journal (brass liner on tailshaft) contains a series of grooves into which lignum vitae blocks were fitted. These provided a bearing surface which was lubricated by the circulation of seawater.

The tailshafts could not be drawn out because of other wreckage, and so the side of the sterntube, supporting bracket and ship's outer hull had to be cut through. This totalled 1-5/16th in of brass, 3 in of cast iron, 6 in cast steel, and 1 in steel plate. Although an individual charge in excess of 10 lb was rarely used, a total of 105¾ lb was used on the port shaft and 137¾ lb on the more deeply buried starboard shaft to recover in excess of 6 tons of gunmetal.

The propeller shafting was supported along its length on tunnel (or plummer) blocks which were made of cast iron lined with whitemetal, the lower shell being the only bearing surface. Those at all accessible were recovered.

Three of the main generators manufactured by W.H. Allen, Son & Co, lay aft of the main engine on the starboard side, while another lay between the shafts. They were of the four-pole type driven by their own steam-engines at 245 rpm to produce 600 amp and 100 volts. The generators were approximately 5 ft long and 5 ft high. The four field coils were separated into pairs by explosives before lifting, and the armature bearings were cut with explosives at either end and divided from their engine flywheel, in order that the armature could be lifted separately. The field coils yielded 2 cwt of copper each, and the armatures 9 cwt each, making a total of 17 cwt of copper from each generator. Only 6 lb of explosive were needed on each to break it into the constituent parts.

Just aft of the thrust block were two enormous cast-iron gear wheels attached to the propeller shafting. Smaller gunmetal worm wheels could be engaged on these for turning the main engines over during maintenance prior to starting. The worm wheels and associated bearings were dismantled and removed as an added bonus.

The thrust blocks were next to be taken apart. These horseshoe-shaped, cast-steel bearings faced with whitemetal transferred the forward push of the propeller when going ahead, and the backward push when going astern, on to the hull of the ship. They were located in position and adjusted by two long brass-threaded bars which ran along either side of them. There were 12 shoes on either shaft, 6 ahead and 6 astern. Each shoe yielded 150 lb of high-grade whitemetal plus, of course, the brass-threaded bars and cooling pipes etc. Extracting them was a difficult job as the whitemetal had tended to fuse on to the steel rings of the shaft. Very small multiple charges were required to free them.

The four 17 ton condensers were each made up of approximately 3,000 ¾ in diameter tubes 14 ft long, encased in a cylindrical brass housing. Two of the condensers had large pieces of engine settled on top of them; in one case the piece of engine was rolled off the condenser with a small charge. In the other the steel was momentarily lifted with a charge, while a split-second later the condenser was rolled out with another—not very far, but sufficient for the piece of engine to slip down behind the condenser. The housing endplates were then blown off using a necklace charge, and the cylindrical housing made up of three cylinders bolted together in the vertical plane was cut horizontally, using approximately 1 lb of explosive per foot length. The charge was tied to a loose condenser tube on the surface, and then laid inside the condenser but firmly pressed against the 1 in brass casing. When the charges went off, severing the plates horizontally, all the bolts in the vertical plane sheered, leaving the top half of the plates ready to lift off. The tubes were lifted out, and then the lower halves of the casing lifted separately.

The four air pumps—of the vertical single-acting type—each yielded 2 tons of gunmetal. A small charge was used to disconnect the pump crosshead bearings, and then 1¼ lb was placed in the lower suction side of the pump. This blew the piston, shaft and top cover out of the pump, also swelling the brass barrel of the pump, causing the surrounding cast iron to be cracked off. The piston, shaft and top cover were lifted as one lift, the pump casing as another. The pump could have been lifted whole, but it would then have posed real problems to dismantle into its constituent parts before selling. The shaft was manganese bronze, the barrel intermediate gunmetal, the piston commercial gunmetal, and the outer casing yellow brass with cast iron attached in places.

Situated close to each condenser was a large centrifugal pump to circulate the seawater as a coolant through the condenser, and then discharge it overboard. The ½ ton central-vaned pump wheel was of gunmetal and keyed to a manganese bronze shaft which was driven by its own small steam-engine. The outside cast-iron casing was cracked away by using two separate charges; the first, of 1 lb, disconnected the pump from its engine and also opened a small inspection hole in the cast-iron housing. Another charge of 1¼ lb was placed through this, cleaning off the rest of the cast-iron housing to leave the ½ ton vaned wheel completely free with its manganese bronze shaft.

Bearings on all shipwrecks present a major problem, and on many ships are uneconomic to recover because of their poor quality. The *Oceanic*'s were of the highest quality, and the sheer size of each big-end shell was 700 lb—600 lb gunmetal and 100 lb whitemetal. This made them difficult to handle and sometimes, after being freed, they became trapped between falling pieces of engine, resulting in more time and work being expended to extract them. A total of 16 big-end shells weighing an overall 5 tons was recovered.

The small-end or crosshead bearing had two pairs to each connecting rod weighing 170 lb each half shell, and beside these were the slides, made up of cast iron and faced with five whitemetal slabs of 14 lb each. They were intended to guide the crosshead as it worked up and down, keeping in line with the piston rod.

The crankshaft main bearings yielded 200 lb of whitemetal from each cast-iron shell. The bearing cap was blown off to reveal the top shell, which was removed and then the bottom shell was spun round with a very small charge to bring it to the top. It was an extremely difficult job, since too much explosive would start avalanches of cast iron which would quickly bury the bearings, making some uneconomic to recover.

There were many small ancillary bearings, which were removed when they proved easily accessible, but time was always short and the economic aspect had always to be borne in mind. This was very true of the eccentric bearings and in this case the small whitemetal bearing surfaces were only moved when they were obviously easy to extract.

The bearings proved to be one of the most difficult parts of the ship to extract, causing many disappointments and much repetitive work. We would like to think that if it were not for the awkwardness of the wreck site we might have had them all!

Just forward of the engines lay most of the pumps and valve chests, including the feed filters, feed heaters, independent feed pumps, bilge pumps, ballast pumps and much auxiliary equipment. Aft of the engine between the shafts lay the two evaporators—used for converting seawater into fresh water—made by the Liverpool Engineering & Condenser Co Ltd, under the Quiggins patent. They each yielded approximately 6 cwt of copper and brass when finally broken down.

Although all the boilers had shifted from their original position, a very common occurrence on exposed shipwrecks, they had left behind them all their fittings, presumably broken off as they rolled out of position. We found most of the fifteen boilers, but not one had retained any of its fittings. The loose boiler fittings recovered included the main stop valves, auxiliary stop valves, safety valves, pressure gauges, water column gauges with cocks, donkey-feed checks, main-feed checks, bottom and surface blow-off valves and many other small fittings and pipes. We even recovered one of the chef's poached-egg pans, his kettle, hot-water pot and tea urn—all copper but twisted and buckled almost beyond recognition!

There were many other fittings recovered, including such common items as portholes, but one sometimes met with pleasant surprises such as discovering the teeth on the anchor windlass were made of brass! Each blasting job would be carefully costed before being undertaken, and I liked to use the figure of £1 for 1 lb of explosives. Although the price of explosives is well under half this figure, I feel it is reasonable because of the security and extra precautions necessary when handling explosive, the work of setting the job up, and the cost of detonators, cable and other small items. The quality of recoverable non-ferrous metal would be estimated, and a decision reached on the viability of each operation. This also meant that we would be thoroughly familiar with the job in hand and would move from one part of the wreck to another so as not to bury an air pump when blasting a bearing! When we considered there was sufficient loose scrap on the wreck we would only then spend several tides lifting with the big boat. This way costs were kept to a minimum, and we hoped to be making maximum use of the available diving time.

Index

Adelaar 170, 177
Admiralty 18, 20, 29, 32, 35-38
Adriatic 17
Aiva II 160
Alis Wood 156, 185
Allen and Son, of London and
  Bedford 153
Alsatian 24
Argyll 197

Beattie, Alan 74
Beattie, Andy 73, 74, 89, 172
Beattie, Edith 74
Blair, Davy 23, 24, 29, 30, 32, 35
Blewett, Mrs Beatrice 144-146, 183
Bountiful 66
Bourne, Ros 131
Buchan, Jim 108

Cameron, Capt J.G. 16, 17
Castor 183
Churchill, Winston 20
Clark, Tommy 174, 177, 178
Coastal Express 119
Cohen, George and Sons 36
Cox and Danks (later Metal Indus-
  tries) 36
Crawford, Moya 163-165, 184, 188
  192
Cunard 30

Davies, Sam 159, 192, 196

Edge of the World, The 91

Fair Isle 21, 42-44, 66, 78, 102,
  105, 143, 160, 167, 171, 184,
  185
fittings, salvage of 99, 100, 152-
  155

Forward 24, 26
Foula 21-24, 26-32, 35, 38, 39, 42-
  45, 50, 59, 61, 62, 66, 68, 72-74,
  78-80, 84, 86, 89-97, 101, 102,
  104, 105, 108-110, 115, 116,
  120, 125-127, 130, 132, 133,
  142, 148, 160-163, 167, 169,
  171, 172, 177, 178, 181, 183-
  185, 190, 191, 195, 197
Foula, map of location 22
Foula, people 164

Gardiner, Lt. 26, 29, 35
Gear, Bobby 155
Gear, Davy 147, 155, 159
Gear, the late Davy 49
Gear, Harry 48, 59, 62, 63, 71,
  79, 95, 96, 104, 163, 172
Gear, Isobel 95
Gear, Jim 49, 50, 54, 61, 132,
  184
Gear, Ken 49, 68, 75, 126, 131,
  132, 159
Gear, Sheila 95
Glenogil 24
Good Shepherd III 44, 79, 102,
  106
Gray, Peter 27
Gran Grifon 167
Grosch, Grizelda 142
Grosch, Peter 142, 143, 162

Haa, the 45, 78, 79, 91, 94, 104,
  115, 124, 163, 168, 169, 171,
  189, 191, 196
Ham Voe 38, 43, 48, 50, 60, 62,
  74, 113-116, 126, 127, 129, 137,
  138, 168-171, 173-174, 178-180,
  185, 189, 195
Happy Voyager 49

Harland and Wolff 12, 26, 193, 197
Hay and Company (Lerwick) Ltd 41, 72, 73, 76, 77, 89, 97, 183, 191
H.M. Customs (Receiver of Wreck) 73, 76, 84, 89
Hoevdi Grund 21, 24, 29
Holbourn, Ann 95
Holbourn, Elizabeth 43, 92, 160
Holbourn, Professor Ian 28, 43, 45
Holbourn, John 95, 141
Holbourn, Rob 104
Hood, William 16, 17

Isbister, Bobby 28, 42, 43, 163, 164
Isbisters (Walls) 80
Ismay, Thomas Henry 11-13, 15, 18, 21

Jamieson, Alfie 156, 185
Jellicoe, Admiral Lord 40
Johnson, Robbie 141
Juna 159

Kilburns Salvage Company 192
Kincora 16

La Morlaye 104
Lerwick 20, 21, 40, 73, 74, 79, 80, 94, 177, 188
Liefde 90
lifting, heavy 108, 111 (diagram) — 115
Lightoller, Commander C.H. 13, 17-19, 26
Lively 195
Long, Tony 167
Loganair Ltd 95, 164, 188
Lusitania 24
Lustre 74, 75, 97
Lyons 26, 44

Majestic 17
Mann, Johnnie 20, 21

Marine Engineer, The 14
McLennan, Kenny 74, 75
Moore, Jack 109-111
moorings, laying 138

Naval and Military Record 29
negotiations with owners 72-74
Night to Remember, A 18
Nordsternen 45, 129
Norseman's Bride 66
North East Salvage and Ship-breaking Co Ltd 36
Nundy, Arthur 72, 73, 76, 77, 81, 84-86, 89

Oceanic (previous vessel of name) 11
Oceanic 10, 11, 13, 15-21, 24-27, 29-32, 35-38, 40, 42, 44, 45, 49, 54, 56, 58, 59, 61, 63-66, 68, 72, 74-79, 81, 82, 84, 85, 89, 90, 92, 104, 109, 118, 124, 131, 132, 137, 138, 141, 144, 145, 155, 162, 166, 171, 174, 181, 183, 186, 189, 191-193, 195, 197
Oceanic diagram of course 25; side elevation of wreck 67; engine room plan 100
Oceanic Steam Navigation Company 11
Oldfield, Chris 153
Olympic 108
Orkney 20, 42

Pathfinder 14
Pilot Us 159
Price, Richard 89, 90
propellers 77, 78, 98, 99, 135, 136, 146, 147, 181-183, 189-191
Provider 156, 159, 161
Prytheric, Maggie 150, 162, 187, 190

Ratter, Andrew 155, 180, 184
Ratter, Francie 95, 127
Ratter, Jim 155
Ratter, Jock 72, 79, 104, 167

Ratter, John Andrew 117, 127, 128, 130, 133, 134, 138, 143, 147, 148, 151, 152, 159, 162, 181, 183, 186, 187, 189, 191, 192, 195
Ratter, Magnie 155, 156
Ratter, Peter and Bessie 155
Ray, Capt Ian 164
Reid, Albert 66
Reid, David 66
Reid, John 79
Robertson (Lerwick) Ltd 40
Robertson J.W. 36, 37, 40
Robertson, Joanne 165
Robertson, Robbie 36, 38-40, 44, 46, 48, 54, 68, 72, 143, 165, 193
Rowden, N., Dept. of Trade 61, 62, 72
Royal Navy 19, 20

St Andrews Institute of Maritime Archaeology 167
St Clair 80, 120
St Kilda 91, 105, 130
St Paul 17
Scalloway 29, 109, 110, 116, 117, 125, 126, 138, 141, 155, 180, 183, 184, 186, 189-191
Scapa Flow 20, 36, 40, 108
Scapa Flow Salvage Company Ltd 36, 40, 72
Scientific Survey and Location Ltd 89, 90
Scott, Walter 141
Scrabster 181, 189
scrap prices 124
Seaforth Engineering 120
search for wreck 46-53
Shaalds 21, 23, 24, 26, 38, 39, 43-46, 49, 50, 57, 59, 60-63, 68, 71, 72, 75, 77, 80, 84, 92, 97, 102, 109, 110, 123, 127, 128, 133, 143, 145, 147, 149, 151, 152, 159, 162, 165, 179-181, 184, 186, 195, 196
Sheriff, Lerwick 79, 84, 86
Shetland Islands 20-22, 27-29, 38, 42, 68, 78, 86, 90, 93, 102, 103, 105, 109, 110, 132, 141, 163, 165, 166, 168, 171, 172, 177, 186, 195, 197
Ship's Log 29-32, 35
Sinclair, Barry 184
Slayter, Captain William 18, 21, 23, 24, 29-32, 35
Smith, Capt Edward 17
Smith, Capt Henry 18, 19, 23, 28-30, 32, 35
Smith, Pat 163
Spes Clara 160
Spray 159
Stamford, Eric 173
Stevens Haulage, Wick 103
Sumburgh 42, 118

Tayport 120, 123, 154-156, 163, 166, 181, 186, 195
Teal Duck 45
Teutonic 17
Timmings, Lesley 131, 132, 138
Titanic 9, 10, 12, 13, 15, 17, 18, 24, 56, 77, 108, 193
Torrey Canyon 56
Trygg 106-110, 112, 113, 115, 118, 119, 123-126, 129, 133, 137, 138, 141-143, 146-148, 151, 154, 162, 163, 166-174, 177-180, 182, 183, 190
Tubantia case 82-84, 86
Tulloch, Magnie 138, 141

Umphray Andrew 39

Valorous 174, 177-181, 183-187, 189-192, 195

Walls 38, 79, 80, 84
Watchful 20
White, Bill 195, 196
White Star Line 10-14, 16, 28, 29
Wrestler 14

Yeoman, Deirdre 105, 114